THE SECRET
According to
JESUS

THE SECRET According to JESUS

Living a Joyful Life

ED TOWNLEY

BROWN BOOKS
PUBLISHING GROUP

THE SECRET ACCORDING TO JESUS
Living a Joyful Life

Front cover design by Wendell Mathews, MDiv, MFA, PhD

An earlier version of this work was published in hardbound in 1997 as *Meditations on the Mount.*

Manufactured in the United States of America

For information, please contact:

Brown Books Publishing Group

16200 North Dallas Parkway, Suite 170

Dallas, Texas 75248

www.brownbooks.com

972-381-0009

A New Era in Publishing™

ISBN-13: 978-1-933285-91-7

ISBN-10: 1-933285-91-5

LCCN: 2007929519

1 2 3 4 5 6 7 8 9 10

CONTENTS

In Appreciation

The Secret According to Jesus is lovingly dedicated, first, to three wonderful spiritual centers in which I was able to develop and define my ideas and understanding of spiritual progress. First, Unity Church of Beaverton, Oregon, for patiently tolerating the erratic learning curve of my earliest years in ministry. Second, Unity in Chicago for seven years of challenge, discovery, growth and delight. And finally, to Unity Church of Dallas and my three valued friends and co-ministers: Ellen Debenport, John Webster, and Kurt Condra. I am so grateful to be a part of that team and that community.

I also want to acknowledge my profound indebtedness to the great American mystic Charles Fillmore and the Unity movement that has developed around his teachings and perceptions of universal spiritual truth. I am proud to be a part of that movement and always eager to learn more and dig deeper.

Many of my ministerial colleagues have shaped, supported—and challenged! —my ideas through the years. I appreciate them all. And Rev. Linda Spencer has added to all of that a dimension of friendship and partnership that I treasure more than I can say.

Finally, my thanks to my new friends at Brown Books, the unceasingly supportive Karen Kelly, and two people whose initial faith made this book possible in the first place, Mike Moiso and Jeannie Lay.

PROLOGUE

If all the writings of the New Testament had somehow been destroyed, leaving us with only chapters five, six, and seven of the Gospel of Matthew, we would still have everything we need to understand and appreciate the powerful and universal message of Jesus Christ. In this passage, known as the Sermon on the Mount, the writer of the Gospel of Matthew carefully sets out the simplicity, power, and practical value of Jesus' teachings. These elements make the message of Jesus as clear and important to us today as it was to his original followers.

In fact, the Sermon on the Mount is the only how-to book we need. It guides us clearly to a life experience that is free of stress and fear, filled with peace, joy, abundance, and a centered sense of oneness with our spiritual purpose.

The message of Jesus, however, goes beyond simplicity and practicality. Based in a very different culture and from a distance of 2,000 years, we may have difficulty recapturing the revolutionary power of His deceptively mild words. They have become so familiar that they may seem like harmless clichés—true, of course, and nice to hear, but lacking immediacy and relevance in our age of turmoil and uncertainty.

And so we ignore the Sermon on the Mount, or we treat it in a patronizing way, while we restlessly buy, read, discuss, and discard an endless stream of new books, each promising to offer the one and only secret we need. The more confusing and alarming life becomes, the more our bestseller lists overflow with books promising to heal our hurts and transform our lives. And many television talk shows are shifting their emphasis from scandal to spirituality, reflecting our own collective concerns.

At their best these "new" books simply restate teachings that Jesus shared with his followers two millennia ago; these spiritual discussions focus on many of the same issues that concerned Jesus and his followers. Who are we, really? What exactly is our relationship to the spiritual power we call God? What is the purpose of our existence? How can we live life with less fear and stress? These are the questions of today—and the very questions on which the Sermon on the Mount is focused.

Jesus, however, did more than teach; he demonstrated the power of his teachings through the events and healings in his own life. He didn't speak of theories and idealistic possibilities; He didn't describe obstacles and hurdles to be overcome before we are qualified to receive our spiritual inheritance. "The fields are already white for harvest," He said. We have only to recognize the potential and act.

The Sermon on the Mount emphasizes the immediate possibility of harvesting our spiritual good. This is what makes it our greatest guide to reaching and enjoying our full potential—the most concise and complete handbook of spiritual truth ever offered. Time and distance have not diminished its radical power. It stands traditional belief on its head, presents the relationship between God and humankind in an entirely new perspective, and challenges every established teaching about how we are to live our lives—and why.

To draw the most benefit from the Sermon on the Mount, we must approach it from a fresh viewpoint. We must set aside 2,000 years of misinterpretation, free ourselves from what we think we know about Jesus and His message, and hear each statement afresh. We must believe that Jesus (to appropriate the immortal words of Dr. Seuss) "meant what He said and said what He meant."

Above all, we must allow Jesus Christ to speak directly to our hearts. In the final analysis, we don't need anyone to interpret or explain Jesus Christ for us. We have the words. We have our own heart awareness. And we have a direct, eternal connection to Jesus through the Christ, the indwelling Presence of God that He demonstrated and from which He taught. It is the Christ that lives in us as well, the presence that poet Robert Browning called "the imprisoned splendor," waiting to be recognized as our true spiritual identity and released so that we can join Jesus Christ in the great work of creating the kingdom of heaven, choice by choice by choice.

"What I have done, you will do," Jesus assured his followers, "and greater works than these will you do, because I go to the Father." It's a glorious promise. It tells us that we can heal every experience of disease, create abundance for every sense of lack, and find joy and fulfillment in the very challenges of life.

But how are we to do these works that Jesus assured us we could do? How did Jesus do what He did? What was His secret? The answers lie in the Sermon on the Mount.

Because it is short and concise, it is easy to read the entire Sermon on the Mount in one sitting. And it is a mistake to do so. Taken at full gallop, the familiar words and phrases skim effortlessly along, raising barely a ripple in consciousness, causing us to believe that we already know all that we need to know about them. The Sermon seems safe, bland, and powerless. Even if we don't know much about the Bible, these words have become part of our consciousness. "Blessed are the meek . . ." "You are the salt of the earth . . ." And, of course, "Our Father, who art in heaven . . ." These have become gentle, reassuring phrases, drained of whatever power they once held.

We do not need to be reassured today. We need to be challenged. We do not need to be lulled to sleep with homogenized platitudes. We need to be rudely awakened to the Presence and Power that lives within us, to the possibility of the kingdom that Jesus Christ calls us to join Him in creating.

The message of Jesus Christ has seldom been fully heard and understood in the nearly 2,000 years since he walked and taught on this earth. He did not teach of God as a distant being of anger, judgment, and punishment. He spoke of our intimate connection to a God of love and empowerment—a God eager to create and express through us.

Jesus spoke often about the kingdom of heaven, not as a distant place to be hoped for after death, but as a state of consciousness available here and now—a consciousness in which we know and act from our Oneness with God, allowing the Power that is God to create the kingdom through our thoughts, beliefs, and choices. "The kingdom of heaven is within you," Jesus said. And again, "The kingdom of heaven is at hand." We must dissolve every sense of separation and awaken to the Presence of God within us so that Presence can create the kingdom through us.

The nature and dimensions of this awakening may not be clear to us when its vibration first appears in our consciousness. It may be that much of what we have been told of Jesus' message feels incomplete and uncomfortable; and yet we cannot deny the power of His Presence, the love and energy we feel when we allow ourselves to focus on Him. We need to know more, not *about* Jesus Christ but *from* Him. There is no better place to begin than with the panoramic vision—and challenge—of these three chapters from the Gospel of Matthew.

In this book we will move through the Sermon on the Mount in small bites, one teaching at a time, maybe even just one sentence. We will try to digest each one carefully, with a full appreciation of its meaning and its implications in our lives today. And we will close each "bite" with a brief prayer, affirming our willingness to receive and express the understanding and loving guidance of Jesus Christ as we surrender more and more of our human existence to the Power and Purpose of God.

The Twenty Most Important Minutes of Your Day

Here's how the book can be used most effectively. Choose a time in the morning when you can *consistently* dedicate twenty minutes to spiritual focus. It might be immediately upon waking or later, perhaps over the first cup of coffee. (It should happen *before* you leave the house; setting time aside at work sounds good in theory, but it's difficult to maintain the commitment on a regular basis.)

Set these minutes apart from the rest of the day. Light a candle or perhaps a bit of incense. Turn off the television and the telephone (or let voice mail pick up calls). Ask your family to honor this time, simply by allowing you to be alone for twenty minutes.

Sit for a moment in silence or, if you prefer, with some gentle, nonobtrusive music playing softly. Be aware of your breathing without trying to change or force it in any way. Each time you exhale, feel yourself releasing any stress or anxiety you may feel, recognizing that these feelings are from either the past or the future—there is no cause for stress in this precise moment. As you inhale, feel yourself breathing in the quiet power of the time and place; feel a sense of peace moving from your lungs and heart into every cell of your body and every thought in your mind. Center yourself in a sense of gratitude for the Power at work in your life and for your willingness to spend this time of spiritual focus.

Now read one excerpt from the Sermon on the Mount, as it is divided and presented in this book. Read it again, this time aloud. Close your eyes and think about what you've read. Is it familiar to you? New? How does its energy feel? What images does it create in your mind?

Keep a notepad or journal with the book, and write down any thoughts, feelings, or impressions that come up. Don't struggle for the perfect word, and don't worry about spelling, grammar, or punctuation. No one but you need ever see what you write. The important thing is to write down the words and images that come to you.

Now read the commentary that accompanies the day's selection. Read the selection itself one more time, noting in your journal any new images or ideas that come to mind.

Next, turn to the Meditation that ends each segment. Read it aloud, slowly, three times. Pause briefly after each reading to absorb it into your physical, mental, and emotional energies for the day. Choose a word or phrase to remember and repeat, bringing the energy of this time of spiritual focus into the challenges and opportunities you will experience throughout the day.

Each evening, just before going to sleep, take a few minutes to write in your journal, noting any times when that morning's spiritual focus had an impact on your day or when that day's lesson expressed in your life. You may think that the pressures and demands of your life simply don't allow you to set aide even twenty minutes each day. But there's a basic spiritual law you need to know—and it works without fail! It's the same law that expresses through financial tithing; it affirms that anything freely given to God is returned to you at least tenfold. Hundreds of thousands of people from all spiritual disciplines throughout the world can testify that the law works in terms of financial giving. You'll find it works equally as well in terms of time. If you freely give twenty minutes each morning to your spiritual awareness, time will work with you instead of against you throughout the remaining hours of the day! You'll move from one commitment to another easily and even joyfully; you may even find yourself with a little extra time for yourself. Try it. I promise it will work for you if you freely give the twenty-minute commitment each morning.

By following this plan, you will move through the powerful, loving message that Jesus Christ wants us all to hear and understand. It's a message of universal love and personal empowerment that is more important and relevant today than at any time in the nearly 2,000 years since the words were first heard, committed to memory, and later inscribed on precious scrolls.

The Universality of the Sermon on the Mount

In the Sermon on the Mount, we find Jesus teaching, not as a scribe who has memorized the Law and can apply it to any situation, but as an avatar, speaking from a centered position of power and inner knowing. This same awareness can be found in every great spiritual teaching.

The Gospel of John opens with this great image: **"In the beginning was the Word, and the Word was with God, and the Word was God."** In the ancient Hindu scriptures known as the Vedas we read: **"In the beginning was the Lord of Creation; next to Him was the Word."**

Later in the Gospel of John, Jesus is reported to have said, **"I am the Truth and the Life; no man cometh unto the father but by**

me." Sri Krishna tells Hindus that **"I am the way. I am the end of the path, the witness, the Lord, the sustainer."** And Buddha said, **"You are my children, I am your father; through me you have been released from your sufferings."**

So what do we have here? One true spiritual avatar and two impostors? No. What we have is a challenge to see *rightly,* to recognize unity, and to set aside ego-dominated judgments and comparisons. **I AM** is the name God declared for Himself to Moses as He spoke from the burning bush. **I AM** statements from highly evolved spiritual beings have nothing to do with their—or our—limited ego selves.

I AM statements link us directly to the Presence and Power of God within us, a Presence and Power that is the same for all of life, wherever and however it may be expressing. Our own **I AM** statements affirm that God expresses as us, and it is from this divine light that Jesus, Krishna, Buddha, and many others speak. Each is speaking from an awareness of **I AM** statements as expressions from the one God we affirm and experience.

The Non-Step, Non-Secret Program of Simplicity and Practicality

Remember, the teachings we call the Sermon on the Mount are completely practical. They do not force us away from our human experience; rather Jesus offers advice on how to live life at maximum efficiency, working with the Power of God as Law.

Understanding how that Power expresses and flows through us allows us to work with it. After all, there can be no conflict of purpose. Jesus Christ calls us to create with Him a New Jerusalem—a spiritual kingdom here on earth that perfectly expresses the Presence and Power of God. Once we have awakened to that possibility, nothing else can satisfy us, or capture our interest. The kingdom is our own spiritual possibility; it's all we could ever want. We just don't always understand how to get there from here.

The Sermon on the Mount does not offer twelve easy steps or seven basic secrets. It doesn't create a hierarchy of mastery, nor does it promise results in thirty days or your money back. It simply and profoundly reminds us that we are all spiritual beings sharing a human experience; and it describes the most efficient way to bring together these two aspects—to infuse the human experience with spiritual power and thus to achieve the kingdom of heaven by allowing God to create it through us.

It is expert testimony from Jesus of Nazareth, who became Jesus the Christ. He calls us to reach our own Christ Awareness with His guidance and the empowerment of the Holy Spirit.

Let us affirm, as we turn to these great teachings, that we open our hearts to His words, to His example, and to His love.

The Setting for the Sermon on the Mount

The Sermon on the Mount is found only in the Gospel of Matthew. The other gospels include many of the same teachings, often in exactly the same words; but they are scattered through various other times and occasions in the ministry of Jesus. It was the unique inspiration of the writer of the Gospel of Matthew to gather and arrange many separate teachings into the focused dramatic presentation we know as the Sermon on the Mount.

The Gospel of Matthew was written primarily for a Jewish readership. The genealogy of Jesus begins, not with Adam as in the Gospel of Luke, but with Abraham, patriarch of the Hebrew people. Matthew also draws many more connections between the life of Jesus and the writings of Hebrew scripture than do any of the other gospels. The message to a Jewish reader would have been clear: this was the Messiah whose coming was foretold by the prophets.

The Sermon on the Mount occurs relatively early in the Gospel of Matthew, comprising chapters 5, 6, and 7 in the twenty-eight-chapter book. The first two chapters describe the genealogy and birth of Jesus, the adoration of the magi, the machinations of Herod and the flight into Egypt of Mary, Joseph, and their newborn child.

In chapter 3 the adult Jesus is baptized in the Jordan River by John the Baptist, and in chapter 4 he withstands the temptation to misuse His power during his forty days in the wilderness and then begins to gather his first disciples. "And he went about all Galilee," we are told, "teaching in their synagogues and preaching the gospel of the kingdom and healing every disease and every infirmity among the people. So his fame spread throughout all Syria, and they brought him all the sick, those afflicted with various diseases and pains, demoniacs, epileptics, and paralytics, and he healed them. And great crowds followed him from Galilee and the Decapolis and Jerusalem and Judea and from beyond the Jordan."

The ministry of Jesus, then, is still in its early stages at this point, but growing dramatically. Inevitably questions are raised: Who is this guy? How is he doing this healing work? What is his message? To answer these questions, the Gospel of Matthew shifts its focus from what Jesus was *doing* to what he had to *say*.

The Importance of Interpretation

Accuracy of translation is critically important in appreciating the Sermon on the Mount. A slight variation in nuance or emphasis can make a great difference in what we understand Jesus to be saying. At the same time, we have come to expect a high degree of poetic eloquence in these teachings.

I think the best balance of these two important concerns is found in the Revised Standard Version of the Bible. Except where noted, this is the version used for quotations throughout this book.

1

BLESSINGS IN DISGUISE

Seeing the crowds, [Jesus] went up on the mountain, and when he sat down his disciples came to him. And he opened his mouth and taught them, saying:

"Blessed are the poor in spirit, for theirs is the kingdom of heaven.

"Blessed are those who mourn, for they shall be comforted.

"Blessed are the meek, for they shall inherit the earth.

"Blessed are those who hunger and thirst for righteousness, for they shall be satisfied.

"Blessed are the merciful, for they shall obtain mercy.

"Blessed are the pure in heart, for they shall see God.

"Blessed are the peacemakers, for they shall be called sons of God.

"Blessed are those who are persecuted for righteousness' sake, for theirs is the kingdom of heaven.

"Blessed are you when men revile you and persecute you and utter all kinds of evil against you falsely on my account. Rejoice and be glad, for your reward is great in heaven, for so men persecuted the prophets who were before you."

"Seeing the crowds, he went up on the mountain, and when he sat down, His disciples came to Him."

The common picture we associate with the Sermon on the Mount—probably based on biblical films such as *King of Kings, The Greatest Story Ever Told, Jesus of Nazareth*, and others—is of Jesus speaking to a large crowd gathered beneath him on the lower slopes of the mountain. (In fact, it's hard not to think of the Monty Python film *Life of Brian,* in which people on the edge of the crowd are having a hard time hearing: *"Blessed are the cheesemakers??")*

This is not, however, the picture that the writer of Matthew creates. ***"Seeing the crowds, He went up on the mountain."*** Jesus is not plunging into the crowd, or even addressing it, but in fact withdrawing from it. This is one of many times in the course of His ministry when we learn that Jesus leaves the crowds behind and goes up a mountain. He strengthens and centers Himself by ascending to His higher consciousness, from which He can later descend to teach, heal, and minister to the crowd.

"And when He sat down, His disciples came to Him." The Gospel of Matthew was written primarily for Jewish readers. It is in Matthew that we find the greatest number of references to Hebrew scripture, the greatest emphasis on Jesus Christ as the fulfillment of earlier prophecies. Since Jews expected by tradition that a great teacher would be seated to address his students, the image reinforces Jesus' position and prestige. It is also significant that He is depicted as giving the Sermon on the Mount, not to the entire crowd that follows him, but to His disciples in private. Every great teacher in all spiritual traditions is recognized as teaching on two levels: a general level for people at large and a private, more elevated level for his closest followers, his disciples.

Thus the importance of this Sermon on the Mount is emphasized beginning with its first sentence. We are in the presence of a great teacher, and we are to receive not just His general message, but His deepest, most profound teachings. We must realize, as we begin this journey through the Sermon on the Mount, that we are not standing on the fringes of a large crowd, straining to hear a shouted message. We are seated at the feet of the Master, part of a small and select group, and we can easily hear every gentle, powerful word.

MEDITATION

Beloved Teacher, I am ready to hear Your words, to receive Your guidance, to experience Your love. I am quiet and relaxed, perfectly centered and balanced in the energy of my heart. I gently clear my mind of all distractions and all preconceptions. I am open and receptive as the Power of God through You awakens the Presence of God in me.

"And He opened His mouth and taught them, saying: 'Blessed are the poor in spirit, for theirs is the kingdom of heaven."

We begin the Sermon on the Mount with the itemized list of blessed people, commonly known as the Beatitudes. They are the exact opposite of curses; they affirm a positive spiritual energy, the very Presence of God, in those people described. Jesus is explaining that certain groups of people are especially connected with their spiritual potential.

The familiar translation "blessed are" does not match the energy of these statements. Other translations have substituted "happy are" or "favored are" with little benefit. The more recent Scholar's Version captures both the meaning and the energy with a jolting choice of words: "Congratulations to the poor in spirit, for theirs is the kingdom of heaven!"

The word "congratulations" helps us to grasp how radical and dangerous these Beatitudes must have seemed when they first were expounded. At this time people learned and believed that wealth, happiness, and success were all signs of God's favor. People who were poor, sick, or failing in any way were clearly being punished by God. Then along comes Jesus, offering his spiritual congratulations to the very people who were being judged and condemned by the religious authorities of the time. He is telling those who have been most thoroughly excluded from religious acceptance that they are, in fact, God's beloved. What an energy of hope and new possibility His words must have carried to the sick and needy who thronged to hear Him!

In this, the first of the Beatitudes, to be poor in spirit has nothing to do with lacking money or possessions. I have often felt most poor in spirit at times when money was more or less abundant, perhaps because I allowed the money to become a distraction, at the cost of any spiritual focus in my life.

To be poor in spirit is to feel dissatisfied with material things, no matter how abundantly they may be expressing in our lives. Someone poor in spirit lacks the realization that there is a higher dimension to life than material things. The rich are poor in spirit if they focus on the material goods they've accumulated. And the poor are poor in spirit if they focus on the material goods they don't have. We cannot begin to explore our spiritual possibilities until we recognize something more important than wealth and possessions. This hunger for a deeper experience of life, the nagging sense that the material world alone is not enough, is the essential first step on the path to the kingdom.

This is why the poor in spirit are so blessed: they have begun to awaken from the illusion that material success is the only goal worth achieving and to recognize a different calling deep in their hearts. They may be young or old, rich or poor. They may have come to their awakening through years of study, through extensive life experience, or through a sudden, overwhelming moment of realization. Whoever and wherever they are, and whether they know it or not, their new sense of spiritual poverty represents the first step on a great personal adventure from which there is no turning back.

This first step can be scary, since few of us realize at the time exactly what's happening. That's why this first promise of Jesus' great discourse is so important: ***"Theirs is the kingdom of heaven."*** In other words, once the spiritual journey is begun, its successful completion is assured. There's no chance of failure, because God is eternally seeking us even more eagerly than we are seeking God. We *will* realize the kingdom. Guaranteed!

MEDITATION

Today I give thanks for the sense of dissatisfaction that leaves me feeling poor in spirit. I recognize that this restlessness is the first step of a personal journey of discovery and empowerment—a journey without distance that will allow me to realize and experience my Oneness with all that God is.

"Blessed are those who mourn, for they shall be comforted."

Jesus often warned that the spiritual transformation to which He called His followers required so much change, so much "letting go" of old attitudes and customs, that it might often feel like an experience of death. Our new commitment to God, he said, will sometimes separate us from family, friends, and everything familiar. Take up your cross, he invited, and follow me.

It isn't an appealing invitation. And yet it's comforting to know that the grief of separation is an integral, intimate part of each true journey.

Spiritual transformation is a constant process of letting go. We relinquish our hold on people, places, and things as we realize that they are neither the problem nor the solution. The Presence and Power of God are all we need or want, and God is always with us; there is no need to clutch at anything or anyone.

Yet every letting go gives rise to a deep sense of grief. Not just the letting go we call death, but even the most joyful release of negative attitudes, the most freeing dissolution of jealousy or possessiveness—each time we let go of something familiar we trigger a sense of grief.

This inescapable truth is familiar to anyone who has released an addiction of any kind. I remember, from a distance of some twenty years, the intense grief I experienced when I stopped smoking. It felt as if my very best friend were dying over and over again, on a daily, even an hourly basis. The Sermon on the Mount was far from my consciousness at the time, so I couldn't hear Jesus' promise of blessings beyond the grief. And yet somehow, even though I didn't know to expect it or claim it, the comfort came, the blessings expressed.

My path from that time of releasing addictions (smoking was only one of several) to now has clearly been a path of progressive joy, love, and heart empowerment. And yet I have mourned many, many times, over perceived losses great and small, only to receive unimagined blessings as a result.

How could it be otherwise? It is our human nature to grieve whenever we let go of anything familiar—a relationship, an attitude, a job; even if we are unhappy with the status quo, we grieve its release nonetheless. The only way to avoid grief, therefore, is never to let go of anything. But this means we must close the door on all spiritual growth, since change is its very nature.

The path of enlightenment requires us to mourn, to recognize and honor our grief as we continue to move through it. Mourning leads us from the sense of loss to an acceptance of God's Will and an openness to exciting new possibilities.

MEDITATION

Today I recognize and embrace a sense of grief and mourning in myself as I release old beliefs, behaviors, and priorities. I remember the promise of Jesus Christ that He will send the Comforter, the Holy Spirit, and I receive that comfort now, as I open my heart to new spiritual possibilities. Thank You, Holy Spirit, for the light and love that transform mourning into a profound sense of joy.

"Blessed are the meek, for they shall inherit the earth."

Anyone who has ever been to a Twelve Step meeting is familiar with "How It Works," the excerpt from the Big Book of Alcoholics Anonymous that is read at the beginning of almost all such meetings. It is not a list of orders and rules; it is a careful, loving explanation of what we can do to release old attitudes and behaviors and realize a happier, more abundant life.

The Sermon on the Mount is in many ways Jesus' own "How It Works." His powerful precepts are not about right and wrong; they are not about denying ourselves or limiting our lives. They are guides to understanding how the Power of God works in the world, so that we can consciously work *with* that Power to realize our greatest good.

The first two Beatitudes describe how we begin our spiritual transformation by feeling dissatisfied (poor in spirit) about life as we have been living it, and by experiencing a sense of grief that accompanies any release of old behaviors, old attitudes, old addictions.

Next, says Jesus, **"Blessed are the meek, for they shall inherit the earth."** We don't often consider meekness an admirable trait. The meek are those who do not assert themselves, who avoid conflict of any kind, and who (from our limited human perspective, at least) sacrifice their goals and desires for fear of upsetting anyone else. To be meek, it seems, would be to live in a constant state of weakness, of surrender to stronger forces.

But surrender is just what's required as we set out on our spiritual journey. We surrender our own limited power to a Power greater than ourselves, and we recognize that that Power can carry us to possibilities we could never reach on our own.

We experience that Power in the love and example of Jesus Christ and in the energy of the Holy Spirit active in our human experience. We choose to set aside our own priorities, based as they are on a limited perspective, and accept the guidance of that Power in our lives.

We have been trying to conquer the world on our own power. Now, by surrendering, we inherit the earth. We achieve our greatest good not by struggling and fighting for it, but by allowing the Power of God within to carry us to the good that is our birthright.

MEDITATION

Today, or at least for this moment, I cease to struggle. I release my limited sense of who I am and what I want or need. I recognize the loving Power of the Holy Spirit, and I accept that Power as my only priority. I open my heart to the Holy Spirit, and I "inherit the earth." I richly enjoy my human life as the spiritual experience it is eternally meant to be. Thank You, God!

"Blessed are those who hunger and thirst after righteousness, for they shall be satisfied."

There is an Eastern story about an eager young man who traveled many, many miles to seek out a spiritual teacher who was, he had been told, both holy and wise. When he finally reached the old man, he found him standing in a great river. Fearlessly he waded into the water and approached the venerable man. "Great master," he said, "I have traveled far to find you. Please tell me, how can I find God?" Without a word the sage, with surprising strength, grabbed the young man and pushed his head under water. With increasing panic, the young man struggled to escape but to no avail. Finally, at the last possible moment, the old man released his grip and the young man staggered, gasping for breath, to the shore. Serenely the teacher followed. "What were you thinking just then?" he asked. "Thinking?" the young man gasped, "I was thinking about air! I wanted nothing in the world so much as one breath of air." "When you want God as much as you just wanted a breath of air," the teacher replied, "then God will find you!"

Jesus, in his Sermon on the Mount, said, **"Blessed are those who hunger and thirst after righteousness, for they shall be satisfied."**

Most of us have dabbled at many things in the course of this human experience. We are freer today than at any time in human history to try new things, to sample cultures and attitudes from all over the world. If one thing loses its appeal, many others can replace it. Jobs that were once considered lifetime commitments may be only trial balloons, as we search for the perfect something that will satisfy us. Men and women who would once have been counting the days to retirement are instead embarking upon entirely new careers.

We recognized in the previous Beatitude that letting go causes a sense of grief; but it can also become addictive. Restlessness can become a way of life. Like the Israelites en route to the Promised Land, we may find ourselves in a wilderness experience, grieving for the comforts we left behind in Egypt and unclear about just where we're supposed to be going. After a while, however, the wilderness itself becomes comfortable; the ability to fold up our tents and move somewhere else serves our restless nature and makes it unnecessary to stop, claim our ground, and deal with whatever challenges arise.

Certainly this pack-up-and-move-on mentality is frequently expressed in our pursuit of spiritual satisfaction. We may wander restlessly from path to path, following trends or friends or simply the random guidance of our own curious minds. Indeed, this curiosity is an important characteristic of our human experience.

Curiosity, however, is not the hunger and thirst that Jesus is blessing. We cannot undertake our spiritual commitment as a hobby to be enjoyed in whatever spare time we allow ourselves after the "important" things like job and family are taken care of. We must want to know God—to experience the Presence of God within ourselves—like a drowning man wants air. God cannot feed us if we are not hungry enough to ask, to seek, to knock. When we do, we will be satisfied.

MEDITATION

Today I am eager for my wilderness experience of searching and seeking to be over. I am ready to be still and allow the Holy Spirit of God to satisfy the hunger that leads me to seek Your Presence in my life, knowing it is through that hunger that I come to You, my only satisfaction.

"Blessed are the merciful, for they shall obtain mercy."

Mercy is a much-abused word in the world today. As with many spiritual concepts, we have allowed it to take on a more technical, legalistic meaning than it was originally intended to convey. To "have mercy" today is to either negate or lessen the consequences which people earn as a result of their actions. If I have a valid legal case against someone, I am allowed to consider myself "merciful" if I decide not to press charges.

But that understanding of "mercy" contains a lot of residual negative energy. I am still judging the person to be guilty, even if I magnanimously choose not to inflict the degree of retribution that his guilt deserves. This is a good thing, of course, but it is far from the universal spiritual concept that Jesus calls us to in this deceptively simple beatitude. He emphasizes again and again throughout this great discourse that "blessedness" lies not in the actions that we take, or don't take, but in the consciousness behind those choices.

The word which my Merriam-Webster Dictionary uses, first and foremost, to define both "mercy" and "merciful" is "compassion." And there is no energy of judgment in compassion! The same dictionary defines "compassion" as "sympathetic consciousness of others' distress together with a desire to alleviate it." Pundits and politicians were much amused at former President Bill Clinton for assuring his listeners, "I feel your pain!" And yet that is the essence of compassion—of the quality of mercy that Jesus is describing in this beatitude. We feel the pain of others as we become aware of, and sensitive to, the sympathetic consciousness that we share.

A legalistic interpretation of mercy can still be useful to us if we have made negative choices and need to be relieved of their consequences. But fully embracing a sense of compassion—mercy in its fullest spiritual meaning—takes life to a whole new level of possibility. It removes judgment altogether — judgment of others by me, judgment of me by others, even judgment of myself by myself! A "sympathetic consciousness" allows us to understand that no one is deliberately trying to do evil. The same fears that lead others to harm us exist in our own consciousness as well. When I am willing to love others through their challenges and mistaken choices, I will experience that same willingness in my own life and relationships.

This is the wonderful, peaceful, joyful blessing to which Jesus is calling us throughout his entire ministry. It is not a lifetime spent doing everything perfectly and holding others to account for their imperfections. It is living in a "sympathetic consciousness" that recognizes that we're all spiritual beings doing our best to express our spiritual powers through the density of a human experience. It will never be easy, but it will be much richer and more enjoyable when we release all judgment and allow the quality of mercy to flow freely.

MEDITATION

Today I call upon the Presence and Power of God within me to dissolve every judgment I may feel called to render upon others, or upon myself. I feel my oneness with all of life, and I embrace the shared consciousness that allows all of life to blossom together in spiritual expression. Thank You, God!

"Blessed are the pure in heart, for they will see God."

As with other spiritual terms, "purity" carries a lot of negative baggage. And as with other spiritual terms, that negative baggage is a direct result of our insistence on ignoring Jesus' most oft-repeated teaching, that we "Judge not"!

We have too often in the past judged some people—including ourselves, of course!—to be acceptably pure, in contrast to others who are judged to be impure. Fascists, racists, segregationists of all stripes have self-righteously upheld their own standards of ethnic, racial, or cultural *purity* by shutting out or even destroying those judged to be less than sufficiently pure.

As always, the problem lies not with the spiritual idea, but with our limited human attempts to apply it. In this clear statement of absolute spiritual fact, Jesus again invites us to set aside the complications we insist on manufacturing within and about our human experience and embrace the blissful simplicity of spiritual law in action.

Who are the "pure in heart"? We will never be able to recognize them by applying our limited human faculties of judgment. We can't see, hear, touch, taste or sniff out the quality that fills a person's heart. "By their fruits you will know them," Jesus tells us elsewhere, and the fruits of the pure in heart can be recognized in the energy we feel when we're around them. We don't have to see proof or read testimonials. We know.

More important is the question of how we can be pure of heart ourselves. It seems nearly impossible, because no one is more aware than we are of just how many energies of impurity we have bottled up within us at any given moment!

But stop for a moment, and be aware. Where exactly are those impure energies—those chaotic combinations of faith and fear, generosity and greed, love and lust that seem to be constantly competing for our attention?

They are all to be found in the thoughts of our minds. There is no such chaos at the dimension of the heart. Our heart energy is pure love, pure faith, pure God. So our challenge is not to figure out how to *become* pure of heart. The challenge is to know that we already are, and to quietly center ourselves in that pure heart energy. This belief in our own heart-purity is the faith, small as a mustard seed, that Jesus insists is all we need to achieve the kingdom of heaven.

"Blessed are the pure in heart, for they will see God." Blessed are those who know that the heart of their being contains only the pure essence of God. For in knowing that truth, they will see God wherever they look, reflected in the faces of everyone they meet.

MEDITATION

Today is filled with wonderful opportunities to express, in the face of every challenge, the essence of Divine Light and Love that constitute the only energy at the heart of my being, and to see that divinity gazing back at me in the face of everyone I meet. Today I rely on the pure energy of my heart. And today, wherever I look, I see God!

"Blessed are the peacemakers, for they shall be called children of God."

We are all children of God, creative beings made in the image and likeness of our divine Source. This is the truth of who we are, and it remains true whether or not we recognize, remember, or express it in our lives.

Our "likeness" to God does not mean that God is a physical being as we are, with arms and legs and internal organs. "God," as Jesus states clearly to the Samaritan woman at the well in John 4:24, "is Spirit." It must follow, therefore, that we are also Spirit. Our true spiritual identity, the creative energy of God moving in and through us, is what the writers of Hebrew scripture called "the Lord of our Being" and what Jesus called "the Christ."

Our personal challenge as spiritual beings who have assumed human form is not to find the Christ, or imitate the Christ, or even to worship the Christ in Jesus as an unattainable ideal. "What I have done you will do," Jesus assured us. Our challenge is to remove all obstacles so that our true Christ nature can express fully and completely through us in these human lifetimes.

What are the obstacles? They are our collective error thoughts—ideas of lack, limitation, and separation from God that we have chosen to believe. Our belief in these negative ideas allows them to become the dominant reality in the manifest world. We create the kingdom of heaven by literally "changing our minds." We decide to "cancel our subscription" to negative thoughts, to "delete the files" of limiting ideas we have accumulated in consciousness, and to allow the indwelling Christ Presence of God to fill our hearts and minds with ideas of love, abundance, wholeness, and infinite possibility.

Dissolving the energy of negative ideas is not ours to do alone, of course; it is the work of the Holy Spirit, eager to have us return to a full expression of who we are. Neither do we have to impress anyone else, or convince anyone else, with the Christ Presence within us. If we are doing our part, keeping ourselves a clear channel, others will see it. We will be called children of God, because that is what people will see and experience when they are with us.

This Beatitude, then, does not tell us that we must become peacemakers *in order to be* children of God. We already are children of God. And as we know that and feel its power in the heart of our being, people and conditions around us will become more peaceful, more energized in love, simply because of our presence. And in that new energy, people will see us—and themselves—as the children of God we are.

MEDITATION

Today I choose to place my focus not on becoming or overcoming, but simply on being—on centering myself in the loving energy of the Christ within me, empowered by a joyful infusion of Holy Spirit. In this deep and exciting energy of the indwelling Christ and the incoming grace of Holy Spirit, I find perfect peace, and I joyfully extend that peace today to everyone I meet. Thank You, God!

Know how to [illegible]
to the young
you have to know what
you don't know

"Blessed are those who are persecuted for righteousness' sake, for theirs is the kingdom of heaven."

We spoke earlier of the hunger and thirst after righteousness which will be satisfied only as we set aside all other considerations and focus only on God.

This last of the Beatitudes recognizes that our hunger and thirst may not be shared by others. We have seen that our spiritual quest often seems wrong and even dangerous to our own doubting and dubious minds. How much more dangerous and wrongheaded will we appear to the collective race consciousness that "knows what it knows" based on ideas of lack, separation, judgment, and guilt.

This Beatitude has been wrongly seen as promising a reward after death for pain and persecution suffered in life. It has even been used through the centuries as a kind of spiritual mind control through which people have been encouraged to accept without question conditions of poverty and oppression in this lifetime by quoting this promise of eternal happiness in heaven. That is not what Jesus is saying. The kingdom of heaven, Jesus said, is at hand. It is, He said, within us. He clearly meant us to experience the kingdom of heaven in these bodies, in these lifetimes.

Jesus is trying to explain that those who resist not evil, who hold fast to truth in a nonresistant, nonjudgmental way, are already experiencing the kingdom. From our limited human perspective, they must be suffering and in pain. In fact they have reached and are experiencing a level of unconditional love that can in no way be threatened by the things and ideas of this world.

This does not mean that suffering is good. It means that when we are truly connected to the Presence of God within us, nothing can cause us to suffer. The world may try to persecute us for our righteousness—our spiritual beliefs and connection—but the world does not have that power. If we choose not to be part of the judgments of the world, then those judgments have no power over us.

I am reminded of *City of Joy,* the inspiring book about a French priest drawn to Calcutta to minister to the poorest of the poor—people without homes or possessions who, in his well-intentioned judgment, could truly be said to be persecuted. What he found was that theirs was, indeed, the kingdom of heaven; they were more able to extend love and compassion to him than he was to them. Conditions in the material world could not shake the peace and joy they felt in knowing their spiritual worth.

Sometimes our spiritual priorities may seem to put us at odds with the world around us. Not to worry. Nothing that others may be trying to deny us could ever be more satisfying than the spiritual imperative that we participate with Jesus in the creation of the kingdom.

MEDITATION

Today I affirm that I remain centered and focused on my spiritual possibilities. I release all judgment of self and of others, as I feel the love that is God channeling through my heart and into every cell of my body and mind. I choose to live this day in that energy of love, to claim for myself the kingdom of heaven, and to discover my role in bringing that kingdom into full expression everywhere. Thank You, God!

"Blessed are you when men revile you and persecute you and utter all kinds of evil against you falsely on my account. Rejoice and be glad, for your reward is great in heaven, for so men persecuted the prophets who were before you."

The Beatitudes conclude with a dramatic shift from third person ("Blessed are *they* . . .") to second person ("Blessed are *you* . . .") for the first statement of a theme that will be constant throughout the ministry of Jesus: the spiritual path to which we are called is not an easy one, nor are we likely to win many popularity contests as a result of the work that is ours to do.

The kingdom to which Jesus Christ calls us is "not of this world" (John 18:36), and it will make no sense to those who are not able to fully understand its spiritual power. What we experience as spiritual growth and awareness will seem like sheer foolishness to others. We can't expect to be understood always, even by people to whom we feel closest, and we certainly can't base our spiritual choices on the prevailing opinions of friends or family. Again and again as His ministry unfolds, Jesus warns his disciples that following a path of spiritual awareness and enlightenment may mean turning away from friends, family, and "public opinion."

Jesus' own life experiences demonstrate this unavoidable conflict. When He takes His spiritual message back to His hometown of Nazareth, He is rejected and scorned. And it is frequently mentioned in the four gospels that His own family did not support or approve of His ministry; indeed, they tried forcibly to bring Him back to Nazareth because they believed He must be insane. After all, Jesus was hanging out with every type of undesirable person—tax collectors, prostitutes, Samaritans—and was consistently offending the Pharisees and Sadducees who constituted the "ruling élite" of

His time. No wonder His nervous family wanted to throw a damper on the revolutionary message He was preaching. Such intense opposition must be expected, Jesus assures us. In fact we should recognize it as a sign that we are doing our spiritual jobs. Our reward will be great in heaven—a state of consciousness that already exists within us. In other words we will find the rewards of our spiritual choices in ourselves, not in the support or approval of others.

MEDITATION

Today I release all anger and judgment in myself as I recognize the opposition and resistance I may receive from friends and family and begin to base my life choices on a new understanding of spiritual Truth. I am called to be a prophet—to recognize and share the spiritual dimension behind each life experience. Any negative energy I may experience as a result strengthens my resolve and centers me in the indwelling Presence of God. Thank You, God!

DOC CHILDRE
HEART MATH SOLUTION

Go to the heart
find the freeze frame
of serenity
Bring it back
to the moment

2

KNOWING WHO YOU ARE

You are the salt of the earth; but if salt has lost its taste, how shall its saltiness be restored? It is no longer good for anything except to be thrown out and trodden underfoot by men.

"You are the light of the world. A city set on a hill cannot be hid. Nor do men light a lamp and put it under a bushel, but on a stand, and it gives light to all in the house. Let your light so shine before men, that they may see your good works and give glory to your Father who is in heaven.

"Think not that I have come to abolish the law and the prophets; I have come not to abolish them but to fulfill them. For truly, I say to you, till heaven and earth pass away, not an iota, not a dot, will pass from the law until all is accomplished. Whoever then relaxes one of the least of these commandments and teaches men so shall be called least in the kingdom of heaven. For I tell you, unless your righteousness exceeds that of the scribes and Pharisees, you will never enter the kingdom of heaven."

"You are the salt of the earth. But if salt has lost its taste, how shall its saltiness be restored? It is no longer good for anything but to be thrown out and trodden underfoot by men."

Salt has been a precious commodity throughout history. Unlike oil or coal or other raw materials, its importance does not lie in what it can become but simply in what it is. It does not have to be burned or processed in any way. It serves its purpose by simply allowing its defining quality—its *saltiness*—to express.

What does it mean, then, to be told that we are the salt of the earth? Just as salt enhances the flavors of everything to which it is added, our true spiritual nature enhances all the essential "flavors" of this human experience. Life is richer, tangier, tastier when we allow our own true nature—our *saltiness* to express.

"But if salt has lost its taste, how shall its saltiness be restored?" The unique taste of salt is its very purpose. Without that it can no longer even be said to be salt. And yet we often seem to lose the ability to recognize our own *saltiness*—the one essential quality that defines us, describes us, makes us unique.

What is that essential quality? It is the inner light, the Christ Presence of God within us that is our true spiritual identity. Have we actually lost it? There are those who would say we have, that the meaning of the story of Adam and Eve is that we have been forcibly separated from our spiritual unity with God, driven from the garden for disobedience. Jesus, however, apparently does not share that view; "You are gods!" he tells his followers (John 10:34) —not "You were gods" or "You could be gods." What's the problem, then? Why do we so often feel disconnected from the rich flavors of life, as though we'd lost whatever spiritual saltiness we might once have possessed?

We haven't actually lost anything, of course, but we may have temporarily misplaced our *awareness* of our saltiness, and so the effect is the same. Salt that has lost its saltiness can no longer express its true nature or serve its appointed purpose. So, too, are we unable to realize the purpose of this human experience as long as we have lost sight of our true spiritual identity.

We can believe ourselves to be lost—even damned. And because we are one with the creative power of God, we can make that belief express in every area of life. If we believe ourselves to be totally lost, and if every choice we make in life reflects that belief, then we will indeed create for ourselves a very powerful experience of "lost." It is literally our God-given right to do so.

But the illusions of loss we create, no matter how dark or painful they are, cannot ultimately overcome the truth of who we are. We cannot be anything other than eternal spiritual beings created in the very image and energy of our Creator.

MEDITATION

Today I choose to recognize myself as the creator of my life experience. Whatever I choose to believe about myself will be reflected in every area of my life. I choose to remember and affirm that I am one with all of life, a creative expression of my Creator source. I know that as I allow the truth of God's Presence and Power within me to reflect in every corner of this life experience, I am bringing the kingdom of heaven into perfect expression. Thank You, God!

"You are the light of the world. A city set on a hill cannot be hid. Nor do men light a lamp and put it under a bushel, but on a stand, and it gives light to all in the house. Let your light so shine before men that they may see your good works and give glory to your Father, who is in heaven."

"You are the light of the world." What an extraordinary statement—and how shocking it must have seemed to those who first heard it! Jesus was not speaking to the spiritually sophisticated, but to ordinary men and women. These people had always been taught that "the light of the world" was the Presence of God, distant and wholly separate from the struggles and limits of human existence. The most they could hope for was to live an acceptably blameless life and earn the right to approach the light of the world in the hereafter.

But here, suddenly, is a teacher with a radically different message. You must begin, He says, not by recognizing the almighty power of a distant God but by recognizing the Power of God within ourselves. "Let there be light!" is the first creative commandment of God in the first chapter of the Book of Genesis. And now, in the first book of the New Testament, Jesus is telling His listeners—then and now—that we are that light—we are the creative power of God in expression.

Knowing this truth—that we are the creative power of God in expression—is an essential step on our spiritual path, but Jesus is also quick to state that this knowledge is not enough. Precisely because this new awareness is so greatly at odds with what most of the world has come to believe, our temptation will be to keep it to ourselves. But that is not the purpose of the light that God creates. Light must be out where it can be seen, where its presence can illuminate the darkness. And we cannot keep our new spiritual awareness a secret, hiding it from others and keeping its illumination for ourselves. We must let our light so shine before men and women that they will see it and come to appreciate it.

Why? Why must we let our light shine? Because we have such a unique light that we must be willing to share with those who have no light themselves? Not at all. Rather, we must allow our light to encourage others to find the same light within themselves, just as Jesus was using His light to help us see ours. It is in that energy of sharing the light that we will create the kingdom of heaven—together.

MEDITATION

I AM the light of the world. Through all the events and discoveries of this day, I will remember to pause and feel the warmth of that light, shining always within me, in the very center of my heart. And I will let that light shine forth, without fear or hesitation, as love, appreciation, and guidance. I AM the light of the world.

"Think not that I have come to abolish the law and the prophets; I have come not to abolish them but to fulfill them. For truly, I say to you, till heaven and earth pass away, not an iota, not a dot, will pass from the law until all is accomplished."

We are often tentative, perhaps frightened, when we find new doors of spiritual possibility opening before us. Perhaps a prayer we've been halfheartedly expressing is suddenly answered. Or we may find in the stillness of meditation a new sense of connection to the Power of God that is unexpected and almost overwhelming. Nervously we wonder if we really are ready for the upheaval that this new spiritual energy might cause in our lives.

Simply being in the presence of Jesus must have been unsettling in a similar way. So far in the Sermon on the Mount, He has thoroughly shaken up everything His listeners ever thought they knew about themselves and their relationship to God. It is not the rich and complacent who are closest to God, He says, but the restless and yearning. We are not unworthy sinners; we are, in fact, the light of the world.

This new perspective on ourselves and on God is exciting, but it's also scary. Is everything we ever believed suddenly overthrown by this new energy? What then is left? What firm ground is there for us to stand on? Not to worry, Jesus assures His listeners. "Think not that I have come to abolish the law and the prophets."

"The law and the prophets" is a phrase used to describe books of the Hebrew scripture that Christians would later call the Old Testament. The first five books—Genesis, Exodus, Leviticus, Numbers, Deuteronomy—are collectively known as "the law." "The prophets" includes the books of Joshua, Judges, Samuel, Kings, Isaiah, Jeremiah, Ezekiel, and the twelve lesser prophets. Together "the law and the prophets" represent the beliefs and rules that had been constant through many generations of religious observance. Jesus is here recognizing that his teachings seem to fly in the face of old beliefs. "I come not to abolish them but to fulfill them."

The law and the prophets of our own lives—old beliefs of lack, fear, and separation—are not wrong. They are beliefs that served us well, carrying us to this point where we are able to understand a deeper dimension of our spiritual truth.

Let us consider, for example, the Ten Commandments—the very heart of "the law." When we were wandering in the wilderness, it was enough that we blindly obeyed the letter of the laws; we were not yet ready to understand the spirit behind them. Jesus Christ is now bringing a higher dimension of spiritual understanding. The result is not that we are now free to ignore the Ten Commandments, but that we are able to understand the spiritual energy they represent. We obey them, not because we are afraid of God's anger if we don't, but because we gratefully recognize the loving guidance they represent.

Now that we see more clearly, we may want to change some of the ways in which we have interpreted the law based on incomplete understanding. Jesus is about to give us several examples of how what "we have heard it said" needs to change in the light of His new message. But He does not ask us to abandon the spiritual energy that has carried us this far.

The law will be accomplished when it has served its purpose of guiding us safely through the illusions of duality and fear to a recognition of our eternal unity with the love that is God. And we can be sure that the new dimensions of possibility we continue to discover will always be consistent with the law that guides us.

MEDITATION

Today I remember and appreciate the law and prophets of my own life: the training, beliefs, and teachers that have helped me to this point of new spiritual awareness. I give thanks for their strength and support. And I move forward fearlessly, certain that the new dimensions of understanding that lie ahead will be built on a solid framework. Thank You, God!

"Whoever then relaxes one of the least of these commandments and teaches men so, shall be called least in the kingdom of heaven; but he who does them and teaches them shall be called great in the kingdom of heaven."

Since the Gospel of Matthew was written largely for Jewish readership, it isn't surprising that the author is concerned with the relationship between Jesus Christ, the dominant figure in his narrative, and Moses, the dominant figure in Hebrew scripture. Matthew wants to reassure Jewish readers that embracing Jesus as the Jewish Messiah they had been awaiting would not require them to reject Moses or the great Law he brought to the people.

Earlier in the Sermon on the Mount, Jesus mentioned the kingdom of heaven as the reward for those who are poor in spirit and those who are persecuted for righteousness' sake; He will refer to it many more times in the course of His ministry. Understanding what He meant by the kingdom of heaven is essential if we are to truly hear His message.

In traditional Christianity "the kingdom of heaven" is often presented as a place we can hope to achieve at the end of the world, if we have died without sin on our souls. What makes the kingdom of heaven so desirable according to this understanding is that it is the dwelling place of God. To be in the kingdom is to be constantly "at home" with God, enfolded always in the Power and Love we associate with that divine Being.

Much of this belief beautifully reflects the teachings of Jesus Christ. The kingdom of heaven is indeed that state of being in which we know ourselves to be in the eternal Presence of God.

Yet Jesus never describes the kingdom as distant or difficult to attain. Matthew tells us (Matt. 4:17) that the central theme in Jesus' ministry was "Repent, the kingdom of heaven is at hand." If by that we were to assume he meant that the end of the world was about to happen, we would have to say, from a distance of 2,000 years, that he was clearly mistaken. But Jesus was not mistaken about the kingdom of heaven.

In another situation Jesus explains to his confused disciples that "the kingdom of heaven is within you." The kingdom of heaven is within—now! What is it within us—at hand now and always—that can be equated with "the kingdom of heaven?" Not our organs, tissues, nerves, and other expressions of physical form, for they are not eternal, as the kingdom surely is.

No, if the kingdom of heaven is within us, it must be found in that part of us—call it soul, spirit, consciousness—that is eternal, that is our link to God, that is, in fact, the Presence of God within us. And we will achieve the kingdom when we choose to live in that consciousness, to allow that spirit to flow into every cell, every thought, every life experience.

It is in this personal sense of unity with the Presence and Power of God that we will find the kingdom of heaven. This is the new covenant that the prophet Jeremiah had foretold. No more stone tablets, no blind faith, no obedience out of fear. "I will put my law in their minds, and write it on their hearts" (Jeremiah 31:33).

Now, this does not mean—as Jesus takes great pains to emphasize here—that the Law can be ignored. The stone tablets of the Ten Commandments can be destroyed because the Law engraved upon them is now engraved upon our hearts. We obey, not out of fear, but out of love.

When I chose to stop the alcohol and drugs that were creating addictive paralysis in my life, it seemed like a huge and noble sacrifice—one I had become willing to make, but a sacrifice nonetheless. I made the decision not to drink or take drugs, at that time, because I was afraid of the consequences, just as the early Israelites obeyed the Ten Commandments out of fear of God's disfavor. This is an essential and important step on our spiritual journey, but more lies beyond.

Eventually, fear must give way to love. Today I recognize that I am sacrificing nothing for the sake of my sobriety. Rather, the choices I make are based today in love—love of myself, love of life, love of the wonderful possibilities that exist in my life because I am clean and sober, completely available to the Presence and Power of God.

So, too, with the Israelites. At the limited level of spiritual awareness represented by their time in the wilderness, the most they could manage was blind obedience out of fear; accordingly, God expressed to them as Law, itemized codes of behavior in every conceivable circumstance that told them *what* to do, without concern or explanation as to *why*. It's like the parent of a small child, realizing that the reasons for a parental decision are beyond the child's ability to understand, resorting to an exasperated "Because I said so!"

That child will grow in wisdom and awareness and eventually will choose to obey that parental guidance, not because he or she's told to do so, but because he or she understands the love that lies behind the Law. Recognizing God as Love does not "free" us from God as Law; rather it is by doing and teaching obedience to divine Law from an understanding of divine Love that we truly are able to cooperate with God as co-creators of the kingdom.

MEDITATION

Today I know and affirm that the Law of God and the Love of God are aspects of the same energy—the ***Power*** *of God at work in my life. I give thanks for the blind faith in God as Law that has guided me safely to my present perspective. And I embrace the understanding faith that allows me to appreciate the deeper dimensions of God as Love. Thank You, God, for your Law and your Love in my life!*

"For I tell you, unless your righteousness exceeds that of the scribes and Pharisees, you will never enter the kingdom of heaven."

Scribes were important professional people in the New Testament times of the Gospel of Matthew. Their ability to read and write meant that they copied (or transcribed) the laws and the scriptures of their society, but they did more. They performed duties we equate today with lawyers and judges: interpreting the laws and applying general principles to specific cases.

Pharisees were Jews whose spiritual beliefs were centered in separating the Jewish faith from all else in the world and in strictly obeying the written and oral laws, particularly the purity codes setting forth exact behaviors that were or were not acceptable to God.

This sentence from the Sermon on the Mount, therefore, must have greatly confused Jesus' original listeners. It is as if we were to be told that we must be more versed in law that a lawyer. How can we be expected to know law better than someone who has made it their entire course of study? How can followers of Jesus be more "righteous" than the very people—scribes and Pharisees—who decide what is and is not "righteous" in the first place?

Elsewhere in His teachings (Luke 18), Jesus addresses this question in the form of a parable directed, according to the author of the Gospel of Luke, to "some who trusted in themselves that they were righteous." The parable is about two men who went into the temple to pray. One was a Pharisee, well versed in the law and obedient to it in every way. "God," the Pharisee prays, "I thank thee that I am not like other men. . . I fast twice a week, I give tithes of all that I get." The other man was a publican—a tax collector who was scorned by the Pharisees and all observing Jews because tax collectors were seen as collaborators with the hated Roman occupation. His prayer in the temple is simpler; he simply repeats over and over, "God, be merciful to me, a sinner." It is this second man, Jesus tells us, whose prayer is heard, "for everyone who exalts himself will be humbled, but he who humbles himself will be exalted."

"Righteousness," then, clearly means something different to Jesus than it did to the religious authorities of his time. If obedience to the Law were the full measure of righteousness, then no one could hope to be more righteous than the Pharisees and scribes, who not only knew the Law intimately in their own lives, but defined it for others as well. Something more must be needed if we are to enter the kingdom of heaven.

What is the new dimension that Jesus calls us to? It is clear from this parable that it is a dimension of humility and surrender to the Power of God. And elsewhere in his ministry (Matt. 18) Jesus told His disciples, "unless you turn and become like children, you will never enter the kingdom of heaven."

Children do not understand the Law, of course. They simply live in a purer, clearer awareness of their oneness with God than adults who have allowed the fears and judgments of the world to obscure their relationship with God. We must set aside distraction and return to the simple, childlike truth that God supports and empowers us on our spiritual path, just as a loving parent supports a child learning to walk, talk, and otherwise function on this human path.

"Righteousness," then, is not a matter of blind obedience to the Law. It is about being "right" with God—about seeing our relationship with God clearly and rightly, as if from the perspective of a trusting, loving child. We may not know the Law as thoroughly as the scribes and Pharisees among us; but we can, and must, be more completely attuned to the Presence and Power of God within us than their Law-focused consciousness can be. Through our surrender to the total, unconditional love that is God we will find the door through which we can enter the kingdom of heaven.

MEDITATION

Today I accept the invitation of Jesus Christ to cease all judgment—of myself and of others. My "righteousness" is not to be established in the eyes of others, nor am I called upon to judge the "righteousness" of others. I will enter the kingdom through a deep personal sense of rightness with God—a surrender to God's Presence and Power as it expresses in my life, guiding me gently to my greatest Good. Thank You, God, for the childlike simplicity of Your love in my life!

Making every choice
came from Christ/love
Consciousness.

3

MOVING TO A NEW DIMENSION

You have heard that it was said to the men of old, 'You shall not kill; and whoever kills shall be liable to judgment.' But I say to you that everyone who is angry with his brother shall be liable to judgment; whoever insults his brother shall be liable to the council; and whoever says 'You fool!' shall be liable to the hell of fire. So if you are offering your gift at the altar, and there remember that your brother has something against you, leave your gift there before the altar and go; first be reconciled to your brother, and then come and offer your gift. Make friends quickly with your accuser, while you are going with him to court, lest your accuser hand you over to the judge, and the judge to the guard, and you be put in prison; truly, I say to you, you will never get out till you have paid the last penny.

"You have heard that it was said, 'You shall not commit adultery.' But I say to you that everyone who looks at a woman lustfully has already committed adultery with her in his heart. If your right eye causes you to sin, pluck it out and throw it away; it is better that you lose one of your members than that your whole body be thrown into hell. And if your right hand causes you to sin, cut it off and throw it away; it is better that you lose one of your members than that your whole body go into hell.

"It was also said, 'Whoever divorces his wife, let him give her a certificate of divorce.' But I say to you that every one who divorces his wife, except on the ground of unchastity, makes her an adulteress; and whoever marries a divorced woman commits adultery.

"Again you have heard that it was said to the men of old, 'You shall not swear falsely, but shall perform to the Lord what you have sworn.' But I say to you, Do not swear at all, either by heaven, for it is the throne of God, or by the earth, for it is the city of the great King. And do not swear by your head, for you cannot make one hair white or black. Let what you say be simply 'Yes' or 'No'; anything more than this comes from evil.

"You have heard that it was said, 'An eye for an eye and a tooth for a tooth.' But I say to you, 'Do not resist one who is evil. But if anyone strikes you on the right cheek, turn to him the other also; and if anyone would sue you and take your coat, let him have your cloak as well; and if anyone forces you to go one mile, go with him two miles. Give to him who begs from you, and do not refuse him who would borrow from you.'

"You have heard that it was said, 'You shall love your neighbor and hate your enemy.' But I say to you, 'Love your enemies and pray for those who persecute you, so that you may be sons of your Father who is in heaven; for he makes his sun rise on the evil and on the good, and sends rain on the just and on the unjust. For if you love those who love you, what reward have you? Do not even the tax collectors do the same? And if you salute only your brethren, what more are you doing than others? Do not even the Gentiles do the same? You, therefore, must be perfect, as your heavenly Father is perfect.'

"You have heard that it was said to the men of old, 'You shall not kill, and whoever kills shall be liable to judgment.' But I say to you that everyone who is angry with his brother shall be liable to judgment; whoever insults his brother shall be liable to the council, and whoever says 'You fool!' shall be liable to the hell of fire."

A recurrent theme in the teachings of Jesus is His attempt to encourage people to move from the limited realm of "knowing what they know" into the unlimited freedom that comes, paradoxically, only by surrendering to the infinite Power of God as it expresses in the universe. In fact, the central theme underlying the Sermon on the Mount is the importance of clearly understanding how God as Law expresses, so that by cooperating with the Law we can transform our lives.

Jesus does not claim to be exempt from God as Law, nor is He offering us immunity from its workings. "Not an iota, not a dot will pass from the Law until all is accomplished," He warns His listeners.

In fact, the Law becomes more important, not less, as we grow in spiritual understanding. Primitive levels of blind obedience to what the Law says must give way to a more nuanced understanding of what it *means*.

The "men of old" Jesus refers to were not spiritually aware enough to do more than control their behavior by repressing their primitive instincts of fear and doing what they were told by a higher authority—the essence of blind obedience.

But as we become aware of the creative power of God expressing through us, we begin to see that simply controlling outer appearances or behavior is not enough. Life is consciousness, and if our consciousness is filled with anger, we will reap the negative energy of that anger, even if we never act upon it or even verbalize it.

Certainly changing behavior is an essential step, but it is not the end of the journey. If we restrain our behavior but continue to hold anger in our hearts, then we are judging others and thereby opening ourselves to being judged by others in turn. If we allow ourselves to express our negative judgments of others, even just verbally, we are bringing upon ourselves a negative consequence just as surely as if we had taken action. We must be willing to stop judging, to heal the anger in consciousness, if we are to transfer this fear-based world into the love-centered kingdom of heaven.

MEDITATION

Today I do not simply obey God's Law; I embrace it. I am focused on the possibility of love in every situation, and I am prospered and blessed as a result. Thank You, God!

"If you are offering your gift at the altar, and there remember that your brother has something against you, leave your gift there before the altar and go; first be reconciled to your brother, and then come and offer your gift."

Once again Jesus is offering practical advice on how God works in our lives. It is not, He repeatedly assures us, a matter of outward forms and rituals. The Law that *is* God in expression in the universe works not from the head but from the heart. And it operates only when we are clear, unencumbered, and centered in the energy of love.

Jesus does not say that observing the forms, as in offering a gift at the altar, is wrong or unimportant. But alone it is not enough. If there are areas of unforgiveness in our lives, relationships that are in need of healing, unresolved issues with other people, they will negatively affect our prayer work, our affirmations of healing or prosperity, our rituals of empowerment.

This may seem obvious, but in fact it is new and important. Jesus is saying that we cannot work one-on-one with God and ignore the other people in our lives or even the other people on the planet. The gift on the altar must be free of negative energy; it must reflect a sense of clarity and peace in all our relationships. Then the love of God can express outward from its center in our hearts, with no blocks or distortions caused by unreleased resentment against anyone.

And what are the outer limits of this teaching? Who, in fact, is my brother? Jesus answers that question clearly in the Gospel of Luke (10:30-37) through the parable of the Good Samaritan.

It is one of the great short stories ever told. A man traveling alone from Jerusalem to Jericho is set upon by robbers, beaten, and left for dead. A priest and a Levite, coming upon the scene of the crime, cross the road and pass quickly on the other side. A Samaritan, however, has compassion; he treats the victim's wounds, carries him to an inn, and leaves money for his continued care. "Which of these three," Jesus asks, "proved neighbor to the man who fell among the robbers?"

This may seem like an easy question to us today, but it posed a real challenge to Jesus' original listeners. Priests and Levites were people of great power and authority—both spiritual and temporal. According to the Purity Code that they enforced, there would be grave consequences for stopping to help. Contact with blood and other bodily fluids, or with a dead body, would render them impure and require a process of purification before they could resume their official duties. And since their duties were, after all, in service of God, it could easily be argued that refusing to become involved was the better choice.

Samaritans, on the other hand, were a people despised, descendants of Hebrews who had intermarried with other tribes and peoples and so were considered "impure." Their place in society was strictly proscribed; they were second-class people with whom true Hebrews did not speak, socialize, or dine.

The priest and Levite, then, were strictly adhering to religious law when they crossed the road and passed by; the Samaritan was condemned by the same law as an outcast removed from God's grace and love. But even the lawyer to whom Jesus has addressed the story is forced to admit that the Samaritan, in disregarding the letter of the law, has better fulfilled the spiritual law of love.

Every person, then, is my brother, and every interaction is an opportunity to replace fear with love.

MEDITATION

Today I resolve to look fearlessly and compassionately at all my relationships and joyfully begin the process of healing whenever a negative issue appears. I will remember, in the words of A Course in Miracles, *that the holiest place on earth is where an ancient hatred has become a present love. And I joyfully turn to the Presence of God waiting in the altar of my heart, and I release it to freely express in all of my life. Thank You, God!*

"Make friends quickly with your accuser, while you are going with him to court, lest your accuser hand you over to the judge, and the judge to the guard, and you be put in prison; truly, I say to you, you will never get out till you have paid the last penny."

Jesus frequently teaches in parables and metaphors that serve several purposes. They help clarify the points He is teaching. They make His teachings easier to remember by relating them to familiar images. And they also serve to obscure the full implications of His teachings, preventing them from reaching those who would misunderstand, those who do not, in Jesus' own words, "have ears to hear."

So it is that this passage might confuse someone not attuned to Jesus' meaning. What accused? What judge? And why should I make friends with someone who's taking me to court? Especially today, when courtrooms and trial proceedings are so much a part of our collective consciousness, this doesn't make sense.

Jesus, of course, was not directly addressing the criminal trials and civil lawsuits that distract and entertain us today. He was speaking metaphysically. That is, He was using familiar images to describe a state of being beyond the physical and events not in the outer world but in our consciousness.

"Make friends quickly with your accuser." We all have an accuser, an adversary in our own consciousness, trying to influence us from a perspective of fear and limitation. It is an internal voice that insists on limits and lack, that tells us we cannot accomplish our dreams. If we try to resist or argue with that voice, we are simply giving strength and credence to the error-thought energy. In so doing we allow the adversary in us to establish the terms of the debate, and we cannot win. The judge within us will always rule against us, and we will be held prisoner in lack and limitation until our perceived karmic debt has been painstakingly paid in full.

The alternative? Resist not evil. Make friends with the adversary. Enfold in light and love every accusation and judgment, dissolving these mistaken thoughts in the light of our spiritual being.

MEDITATION

Today I dissolve every adversarial thought within me, replacing it with a sense of God's unconditional love. Thank You, God, for the power of love that heals every accusation in my mind.

"You have heard that it was said, 'You shall not commit adultery.' But I say to you that everyone who looks at a woman lustfully has already committed adultery with her in his heart."

Here again, having assured His listeners that He was not going to abolish the Law with His teachings, Jesus tries to guide them, and us, to a deeper understanding of the spiritual energy behind the Law. In the process He reveals the radical new understanding of "righteousness" that will keep Him at odds with the religious establishment of His time throughout his years of ministry.

Jews at the time of Jesus defined themselves and judged others according to a strict and detailed code of the Law that had been carefully preserved and passed down through many generations. They traced it to Moses and his experience with God as Law that led them out of Egypt, allowed them to survive in the wilderness, and brought them together as a unified people.

God always expresses according to our ability to understand, and at that early point in spiritual development, the Hebrews needed, and therefore received, God as Law. They were not yet ready to understand the deeper dimensions of God's Presence and Power. Like unruly children, they could manage nothing more than simply to do as they were told, without asking or understanding the spiritual Truth behind the directives.

The code of Law, therefore, measured righteousness in terms of actions. The Ten Commandments, the cornerstone of the Law, are concerned with what we should or should not do. All the rules that evolved out of the commandments were also concerned with behavior: what to eat, what not to eat, what to do or not to do at certain times or in certain situations.

This is all important. We are spiritual beings caught up in a shared human experience, and the challenges of that experience often make it difficult for us to remember our true spiritual identity. Firm rules such as the Ten Commandments help us return to spiritual awareness by emphasizing an important aspect of our human condition: actions have consequences!

Positive actions, especially obedience to the guidance of God, have positive consequences; they bring our human experience more in line with our spiritual Truth. And negative actions—murder, deceit, adultery—have negative consequences. Like Cain after he murdered his brother Abel, when we are involved in negative actions, we become "a fugitive and a wanderer on the earth," unaware of our spiritual identity.

Jesus does not deny that actions have consequences. He does not abolish the Law. Rather, He carries us further, to a deeper understanding of our relationship to the Power of God. He introduces us to a new dimension of our relationship with God, one we were not ready to understand until now. We are ready now to know that our thoughts have at least as much power as our actions. The spiritual damage is done when we choose to embrace negative energy and hold it in our consciousness. Thoughts have consequences, whether we eventually act on the thoughts or refrain from acting out of fear.

It's important to note that this new dimension of spiritual awareness does not mean that we are held hostage by every thought that moves through our consciousness. We cannot prevent negative thoughts, such as lust, from drifting through our consciousness; they are part and parcel of our human experience. We can gently brush such idle thoughts aside without damage. Or we can "entertain" them—welcome them, dwell on them, adopt their energy as our own. In that case, we are going to experience negative consequences whether or not we put the thoughts into action.

Thoughts have consequences! This spiritual truth forms the basis for Jesus' new perspective on righteousness. Behavior is important, but true righteousness requires more: it requires a consciousness of our oneness with God, from which only right action could flow.

MEDITATION

Today I affirm that my consciousness is one with God. From all the diverse thoughts that present themselves, I choose thoughts of love, wholeness, and infinite abundance. I empower these positive thoughts with the energy of my heart, and I move forward into a life experience that fully expresses the Presence and Power of God. Thank You, God!

"If your right eye causes you to sin, pluck it out and throw it away; it is better that you lose one of your members than that your whole body is thrown into hell. And if your right hand causes you to sin, cut it off and throw it away; it is better that you lose one of your members than that your whole body go into hell."

It is not just the kingdom of heaven that is within us. The kingdom of hell is also within us, and we are always choosing one or the other.

We have recognized the kingdom of heaven described by Jesus as a state of consciousness in which we fully experience our oneness with God. We create our life experiences from the Power of God expressing through our thoughts and taking form in the manifest world. The kingdom of hell is exactly the opposite. It is a state of consciousness in which we believe ourselves to be separate from God and create a life experience from the fear and loss engendered by this sense of separation.

In truth, there can be no "opposite" to God. We know and affirm that the Power we call God is omnipotent, omniscient, and omnipresent. That means that there can be nothing and no place that God is not; therefore, the kingdom of hell has no reality in truth. It is an illusion; but we can, through our choices, make it a realistic and painful illusion indeed.

It all comes down to our choices, to where we put the I AM energy of God that lives within us. We are always choosing faith or fear, love or judgment. There are no neutral choices; everything moves us closer to heaven or closer to hell.

Many negative choices initially seem harmless, even attractive in themselves. We may tell a "white lie" to achieve what seems to be a worthwhile goal. We may decide that our own sense of comfort is more important than the well-being of others. But no negative choice is even remotely worth the cost of feeling ourselves separated from the Power and Love that are God.

Jesus, in these attention-getting images, is reminding us of the urgent spiritual power of the First Commandment: "I AM the Lord your God, who brought you out of the land of Egypt, out of the house of bondage. You shall have no other gods before me."

Nothing is more important than our relationship to God. Nothing! Yet we create many "other gods" in our lives and put them first, before the Lord of our own Being. Romantic involvements, family responsibilities, career priorities—all these are rich and important aspects of the human experience. But if we make any of them more important than our spiritual purpose, then we are creating a false god and moving our life experience closer to the kingdom of hell.

Jesus frequently uses strong imagery to make important spiritual points. "It is easier for a camel to pass through the eye of a needle than for a rich man to enter the kingdom of heaven" is another example. Our right eye or right hand cannot literally cause us to sin (except perhaps in a grade-B horror movie about evil transplants). Only our own consciousness, reflected in our life choices, can create the illusion that we are in hell. Jesus is not attacking eyes or hands in this passage; he is emphasizing that anything, no matter how cherished and important it may seem, that pulls our focus and commitment away from the Lord of our Being is going to poison our consciousness and move us into a kingdom of hell. We must move our focus from the false gods in the world to the real Presence of God within us to restore our spiritual priorities and return us to a consciousness of heaven.

MEDITATION

I resolve today to be firm in my commitment to our spiritual priorities, and rigorous in removing any power I have given to material things. I affirm that nothing in my life is more important than experiencing and expressing the Power of God. My focus is clear and unwavering, and I see God expressing everywhere in my life. Thank You, God!

"It was also said, 'Whoever divorces his wife, let him give her a certificate of divorce.' But I say to you that everyone who divorces his wife, except on the ground of unchastity, makes her an adulteress; and whoever marries a divorced woman commits adultery."

For obvious reasons, this is probably the least quoted of all the teachings of Jesus. If we were to remove from our churches all those who are divorced or remarried, few adults would be left in the pews—or in the pulpits.

It is tempting to explain away these statements by casting doubt on whether Jesus ever really said them. Many scholars believe they were in fact added later, in the early years of the Church, to specifically address issues that had arisen among some followers of Jesus Christ. It had become increasingly important to distinguish the new Christian movement from its Jewish roots, and this absolutist view of marriage and divorce was clearly one way to do so.

That may well be true. Certainly none of the gospels was intended to be accurate, objective history; the words of Jesus were not carefully transcribed as He spoke, but filtered through the memories of His listeners and written down some fifty years later.

But to brush aside this or any particular teaching simply because we are uncomfortable with it is the ultimate cop-out. From this and other gospel passages we see that Jesus had a clear and distinctive perspective on marriage—one that His followers tended to remember after he was gone. And there must, therefore, be a spiritual lesson for us in the words ascribed to Him and included in scripture.

Jesus has already told His listeners that their thoughts were as important and had as much power, as their actions. His new understanding of the Law required them to be as vigilant about thought as the Law of Moses had asked them to be about actions. Now He is moving to another concern: the power of our words.

As in the passage that immediately follows this one, Jesus is urging his listeners to be careful about commitments they make before God. They cannot be made and broken easily—not if we invoke the Presence and Power of God within us to witness our vows. Our words, like our thoughts, have spiritual power behind them.

"What God has joined together," Jesus says in Chapter 10 of the Gospel of Mark, "let not man put asunder." The Power of God within us cannot be trifled with. When we invoke that Power, we are linking our words to eternal spiritual truth. That linkage cannot be dissolved easily.

It's also true that the linkage between our words and the indwelling Power of God cannot easily or lightly be made in the first place. In the case of a marriage, we may come to realize that there was, in fact, no joining together in God because one or both people involved were not making a true spiritual commitment. No one can truly believe, for example, that Jesus would expect a woman to remain in an abusive, possibly dangerous marriage. The Power of God cannot bind anyone or anything to negativity. God is love, and where love is absent, there cannot be a sacred union.

Nonetheless, Jesus' warning against casual divorce is important for our spiritual growth. A true spiritual commitment of any kind cannot be dismissed easily when it becomes uncomfortable. Such commitments are to be entered into carefully; and it is only by holding firm to the "I AM" of our commitment that we will reap the spiritual rewards it offers.

The kingdom of heaven cannot be created with impulsive choices made and unmade according to the day's convenience. When we come to truly know the Presence of God within us, we must also know that our words, thoughts, and actions are creative expressions of God. By choosing prayerfully and holding to the spiritual energy of those choices, we will see the kingdom come to be.

MEDITATION

I resolve today to choose my commitments carefully, recognizing that the creative Power of God acting through me imbues my words, thoughts, and actions with the eternal energy of our true spiritual identity. I am knowingly and lovingly creating the kingdom, one choice, one commitment at a time. Thank You, God!

"Again you have heard that it was said to the men of old, 'You shall not swear falsely, but shall perform to the Lord what you have sworn.' But I say to you, do not swear at all, either by heaven, for it is the throne of God, or by the earth, for it is his footstool, or by Jerusalem, for it is the city of the great King. And do not swear by your head, for you cannot make one hair white or black. Let what you say be simply 'Yes' or 'No'; anything more than this comes from evil."

"Keep it simple!" is one of the most popular mantras of the recovery movement—and one of the most challenging. We are so good at complicating our lives, at getting deeply enmeshed in the dramas around us!

We are spiritual beings having a shared human experience. This means that, as Shakespeare long ago explained, we are all actors playing roles. Until recently, most of us were so caught up in the drama that we forgot we were acting, and we passionately believed that the apparently epic struggle going on around us was our true reality.

Accordingly we engaged all the energy we could muster in the struggle of life. We made alliances, swore loyalties, plotted and manipulated like master politicians. Above all, we called upon the great Power of God to enter the fray on our behalf. It's as if we had begun a challenging board game like Monopoly or Risk or Diplomacy, only to get so caught up that we forgot it was a game and truly believed that our whole identity was engaged in every roll of the dice.

I remember a wonderful scene in the Laurence Olivier film version of Shakespeare's "Henry V" that illustrates the importance of where we place our perspective. At first, in close-up shots, we are in the midst of a great battle. Swords are flashing, soldiers are struggling and dying. The sounds are terrible and a gray haze of dust fills the air.

The camera pulls back, and we realize that we are not on a battlefield in France, but in an Elizabethan theatre in London. The "soldiers" are actors creating the illusion of battle and, as the camera continues to pull back, we see that except for the frantic and dusty stage activity, it is a gloriously beautiful and peaceful day. Perspective is everything.

It is the longer perspective that allows us to stop trying so hard to win battles that are only illusions. From the more limited perspective of "men of old," it was important to fight the battle by swearing oaths, making bargains with God, and then keeping those bargains at all costs. But a greater perspective shows that we do not need to swear, to bargain, to sweat and strain for victory.

"From a distance," as Bette Midler sang in her hit recording, everything looks simpler. We don't need to immerse ourselves in the minutiae of the drama. We are not powerless puppets acting out a script that's imposed on us; we are creators. With a simple "yes" or "no" we transform the mundane drama into an expression of the kingdom. We simply have to remember who we are.

MEDITATION

Today I will remember that whenever the immediate challenges of life threaten to overwhelm me, a wider, truer perspective is immediately available. I choose to see the dramas of my life from the perspective of God, easily and joyfully making the creative choices that transform every challenge into an expression of the kingdom. Thank You, God!

"You have heard that it was said, 'An eye for an eye and a tooth for a tooth.' But I say to you, do not resist one who is evil. But if anyone strikes you on the right cheek, turn to him the other also; and if anyone would sue you and take your coat, let him have your cloak as well; and if anyone forces you to go one mile, go with him two miles. Give to him who begs from you, and do not refuse him who would borrow from you."

Once again Jesus is taking his listeners beyond the well-established standards of the Law into a new dimension of spiritual understanding. He has already emphasized the importance of thoughts and words in creating a consciousness of righteousness. Now He turns to the importance of right actions.

Not all actions allowable under the Law are right and appropriate for our new level of awareness. "An eye for an eye and a tooth for a tooth" is sufficient for a primitive level of justice when we are struggling through the wilderness dimension of our human adventure. If we are to continue to grow into a full expression of the Power of God, however, we must embrace a new perspective. We must understand the spiritual power of nonresistance.

Of the several examples Jesus uses in the passage, one in particular would have shocked and confused His original listeners. The land of Israel at the time Jesus spoke was under the domination of Rome; evidence of this foreign occupation was everywhere, causing much anger and resentment among Jews who were nonetheless powerless to act against it.

One of the most hated conditions of Roman occupation was that the Roman soldiers, as they marched across the land, could legally force any Jewish male to carry the soldier's pack for a distance of one mile. Jews understandably found the forced labor to be humiliating, but they were unable to refuse or resist. Their own Law was powerless in the face of greater Roman might.

Jesus responds to the situation by emphasizing the power of nonresistance. Instead of begrudging the Roman soldier the mile of service that he demanded, go two miles instead. The first mile may be forced, but the second will be a freely given gift.

Now the energy of the situation has completely shifted. The soldier, who had been dominant thanks to the power of Rome, is now the recipient of a gift, thanks to the power of love. And the downtrodden victim has become a gracious gift-giver, an expression of the love that is God.

Nonresistance remains a powerful political attitude in the world today, and it represents the clearest path to the kingdom in our individual lives as well. We know and affirm that the only energy at work in the world is the Power of God. When we surrender our own attempts to struggle and resist, and instead focus on allowing God to express through us, the stress and strain of life are instantly eased. Instead of wasting time and energy on resentment and anger, we gain the infinite strength and serenity of God.

Nothing is more damaging to our strength and well-being than allowing stress and anger to block us from feeling the power and joy of God's love. We never have to allow anyone or anything to create that block; by allowing God's eternal Presence to express, we will always prevail.

MEDITATION

Today I will "resist not" the appearance of evil in my life. I know and affirm that God is the only Power, present in every challenge, and I surrender to that Power, allowing it to dissolve resistance, anger, and stress. The love and guidance of God lead me always to my greatest good. Thank You, God!

"You have heard that it was said, 'You shall love your neighbor and hate your enemy.' But I say to you, love your enemies and pray for those who persecute you, so that you may be sons of your Father which is in heaven; for He makes His sun rise on the evil and on the good, and sends rain on the just and on the unjust. For if you love those who love you, what reward have you? Do not even the tax collectors do the same? And if you salute only your brethren, what more are you doing than others? Do not even the Gentiles do the same?"

Here again is Jesus as Master Teacher, using what seems to be His favorite teaching technique: "You have heard it said . . . but I say to you . . ." This structure emphasizes that we cannot simply hammer new teachings into place and expect them to express in our lives; we must first remove the older, more limited belief that previously held us in its thrall.

At earlier levels of spiritual awareness, when we were not yet ready to remember the full dimensions of our Oneness with God, simple rules of survival were all we could handle: love your neighbor, hate your enemy. There is a certain degree of spiritual power in even those basic concepts. By loving our neighbors we give support to the idea of *neighborliness,* causing it to grow and flourish in the world. And by hating our enemies, we choose not to focus on forces that do not have our good at heart.

This simple application of Law gets us through that level of awareness in one piece. But as we move forward, we must also be open to new dimensions of spiritual understanding. Now we're ready to understand that there are more efficient ways of working with the Power of God within us, sending it forth to create ever greater expressions of love.

The Power that is God does not "hate" Its enemies; the beauty and richness of this world are not given to certain people and denied to others. If we are truly to express ourselves as the children of God we truly are, we will not try to destroy our enemies with our hatred, but rather transform them with our love.

We may wonder what tax collectors have to do with all of this, but to Jesus' immediate listeners the meaning would have been clear. Tax collectors were universally scorned in Jewish society at the time. They were Jews who worked for the hated Romans, collecting taxes for Rome from their fellow Jews. And "gentile" was the term used to describe nonbelievers. When Jesus says that even these people are able to extend conditional love if they know they'll get something in return, He is making it very clear that something more is asked from the spiritually aware.

What is asked is that we surrender the idea of reciprocity. We are to love each other unconditionally, as God loves us unconditionally. God does not judge us. God loves us as the spiritual beings we are in Truth. God's love is not affected by the positive or negative details of our human life experiences. God loves us unconditionally. God's light and love are available to us always and infinitely to heal, bless, enrich, and empower our lives.

Why, then, does it often seem that we are being punished for our "sins," for our negative energy? Simple. It is not God judging us. It is not the Lord of our Being demanding retribution. We are judging ourselves. We "hate" ourselves, or at least the imperfect human parts of ourselves, and we find ourselves deserving of punishment. How much more can we accomplish by replacing the hatred with love!

God loves us enough to share with us the power of creation, even when what we create has its source in hatred and fear instead of in the equally available love of God. And so our self-judgments express as illness, lack, and limitation.

If the source of our problems is in ourselves, so is the solution. If we love unconditionally and decline to judge ourselves or others, we are aligning ourselves with the power of God, and we thereby create the kingdom, a human experience that perfectly expresses the love that is God.

MEDITATION

Today I resolve to see myself and others from the perspective of God and to respond with love to every challenge. I begin by embracing those parts of myself that I have spent too much energy in "hating." I enfold all of me—my physical form, my mental attitudes, my emotional reactions—in the warmth of God's love. Thank You, God.

"You therefore must be perfect, as your heavenly Father is perfect."

Apparently Jesus is putting a heavy load on us. Many children or rebellious adults have had this directive held before them, challenging them to measure the distance they have fallen from the demanding standard set by our greatest teacher.

If we must be "perfect" in the sense of making no mistakes, having no imperfections, then we are all destined to fall far short of expectations, at least in this lifetime. This directive cannot be made practical within our human experience, and Jesus quite clearly intended His teachings to be of immediate practical value. There must, then, be another way to understand this teaching and apply it to our human experience.

In the comparable passage in the Gospel of Luke (6:36), the instruction is to be compassionate as God is compassionate, and this helps us understand the teaching and its context. Jesus has just spoken extensively about how we are to relate to each other. We are to be compassionate—to have *passion with* each other and thus to recognize our spiritual unity. That sense of total unity is the perfection of God that we are called to express.

When He speaks, as He often does, of our heavenly Father, Jesus is not referring to a distant God. Our heavenly Father is within us. "It is the Father within," Jesus says elsewhere, "that does the work." And God is not perfect in the sense we use the word "perfect" in describing a person or thing. Perfection from a human perspective is the presence of all good qualities and the absence of all bad. A perfect rose, for example, has the color, scent, shape, and beauty of a rose without any sense of disease or decay. "Perfection" is a concept of our dualistic human existence, since by its very definition it involves both positive qualities that are present and negative qualities that are absent.

The perfection of God is a different thing. God is the One Presence and One Power present in all of the universe. God is the energy that is everything. God is that which is greater than any attempt to define it. God is present in all things—even those things which, to our limited human perspective, are presently expressing imperfectly. God is present within us as our very spiritual Truth on those days when we most feel ourselves expressing Spirit, and God is equally present on those days when we feel most distant from Spirit. The Presence and Power of God is beyond all limitation and all duality, including the duality of good and evil. God exists in a realm of total unity.

To say God is perfect is to say that God is complete, God is All. And this is the sense in which we, too, are to be perfect. It is useless to strive for perfection in worldly terms—through relationships, work, possessions, status. We may achieve these goals, but we'll find that they alone cannot empower us to feel that sense of completion and wholeness within ourselves and with all others that may truly be called perfect. "Seek ye first the kingdom," Jesus said. Seek first to feel whole and complete through the indwelling Presence of God.

And the path to the kingdom is through knowing ourselves as the perfect expressions of God we truly are. Many believe that a spiritual commitment means that we must focus relentlessly on our failings and shortcomings. But if we do that, we are simply creating more failings and shortcomings, because it is the creative law of the universe that whatever we focus on grows. How much more joyful and effective it is to focus on our spiritual wholeness, our unity with God and with each other, and allow that spiritual perfection to grow in every area of our lives.

MEDITATION

Today let us release our own sense of limitation and allow ourselves to feel and appreciate the sense in which Jesus calls us to be perfect—a sense in which we are whole and complete in our Oneness with all that God is.

4

KEEPING A SECRET

Beware of practicing your piety before men in order to be seen by them; for then you will have no reward from your Father who is in heaven.

"Thus, when you give alms, sound no trumpet before you, as the hypocrites do in the synagogues and in the streets, that they may be praised by men. Truly, I say to you, they have received their reward. But when you give alms, do not let your left hand know what your right hand is doing, so that your alms may be in secret; and your Father who sees in secret will reward you.

"And when you pray, you must not be like the hypocrites; for they love to stand and pray in the synagogues and at the street corners, that they may be seen by men. Truly, I say to you, they have received their reward. But when you pray, go into your room and shut the door and pray to your Father who is in secret; and your Father who sees in secret will reward you."

"Beware of practicing your piety before men in order to be seen by them; for then you will have no reward from your Father who is in heaven. Thus, when you give alms, sound no trumpet before you, as the hypocrites do in the synagogues and in the streets, that they may be praised by men. Truly, I say to you, they have received their reward. But when you give alms, do not let your left hand know what your right hand is doing, so that your alms may be in secret; and your Father who sees in secret will reward you."

Here we have another simple, practical, and loving lesson in understanding and applying spiritual law. Again we must remove the interpretations of judgment and fault-finding that have sprung up around this passage and experience it as the helpful guide Jesus intended it to be.

Good deeds do not go unrewarded, Jesus is telling us; but our reward will express according to our intent. If we give alms to the poor because we want to impress people with our giving, we will achieve that goal. The people we cause to notice our giving will be suitably impressed. But because our purpose was shallow, our goodwill likewise will have no depth. There will be no gain in the spiritual dimension.

But if we give secretly, solely to express the love and abundance of God, then our spiritual reward will be in the same coinage of love and abundance, and it will be great. The choice is ours. The Law simply states that where our purpose is, there will our reward be as well.

The Law of Moses which, as we have seen, Jesus often cites, beginning with the words "you have heard it said," is based on the spiritual Truth that actions have consequences. Negative actions create negative consequences. Because this is spiritual law, it is eternally true. It cannot be avoided or dissolved; negative actions always will produce negative consequences.

That simple understanding of basic spiritual law was enough to get the Israelites through the wilderness; and it gets us through many of our own personal wilderness experiences as well. If we stop our negative actions—addictions, compulsions, fear-based habits of a lifetime—we will relieve the negative results that prove so painful.

I remember an "old-timer" in the recovery program of Alcoholics Anonymous who was approached after a meeting by a new member, who had been trying to stay sober for many years without success. "I just don't get it," the unsuccessful one sighed. "We both started this program at the same time, but I haven't been able to stay sober for more than a few days, while you have such solid sobriety and such a happy life. I just don't understand."

"It's really very simple," the old-timer replied. "When I want to get drunk, I don't; when you want to get drunk, you do!" Actions have consequences, and the act of changing actions changes the consequences.

But now we are called to do more than avoid negative consequences. We are called to make positive choices that will begin to express in the world as the kingdom of heaven. This requires that we expand our spiritual awareness to absorb a new understanding: thoughts also have consequences. We may do the "right thing," as in giving tithes to the temple, but it is our unspoken purpose that will determine the results.

If we give so that other people will see us giving, or out of fear of how it will look if we don't give, we will temporarily achieve our goal. But the fear, or the need to impress, will never leave us because we will not be growing spiritually; we will not be moving toward the kingdom.

If, instead, we give freely and joyfully, caring only that our giving be known to the Father, the Spirit of God within us, then our rewards will be spiritual as well. There will be no fear and no false pride. We will receive as we gave—freely and joyfully—from the infinite abundance of the Christ Spirit within us.

MEDITATION

Today I choose to receive and appreciate love and abundance on the spiritual plane, where everything I truly desire can be found. I will seize every opportunity to quietly and privately give patience, gratitude, love, and abundance from my heart, knowing that my rewards will be great in the rich joys of Spirit. Thank You, God.

"And when you pray, you must not be like the hypocrites; for they love to stand and pray in the synagogues and at the street corners, that they may be seen by men. Truly I say to you, they have received their reward. But when you pray, go into your room and shut the door and pray to your Father who is in secret. And your Father, who sees in secret, will reward you. And in praying, do not heap up empty words as the Gentiles do, for they think they will be heard for their many words. Do not be like them, for your Father knows what you need before you ask Him."

Jesus is here applying to the focus of prayer exactly the same expression of Law that he earlier applied to tithing: Where our purpose is, there will our reward be as well. If our purpose in praying is to impress people with our piety, that, and only that, will be our reward. If we seek first the kingdom, if our primary prayer purpose is to affirm our intimate connection to God, that will be our reward, and all our needs will thereby be met.

Why? Will our prayers be successful because we have neatly enumerated our needs to God? No. Will we so impress God with the words we choose that God will change the divine purpose of our lives and give us things that would otherwise have been withheld? No, emphatically not.

The Power that is God is never withholding anything from us at any time. God is eternally creating the spiritual substance that is the only true reality. We form that substance, through the power of our thoughts, into the gifts and challenges that we experience as life. Prayer does not change this creative process, nor does it change its source, God. Prayer lifts our thoughts to their highest level of vibration, so that the experience we create for ourselves reflects the eternal good that is always God's will.

We have simply accessed the indwelling Presence of God, allowing it to flow unimpeded. And since “It is the Father’s good pleasure” to give us the kingdom, it is the kingdom we receive through the power of appropriate prayer.

Keep it simple, keep it clear, and above all, keep the focus on God. This is the energy with which Jesus recommends that we pray.

MEDITATION

Today I will keep my prayer focus solidly on my relationship with God. I will not clutter the prayer picture by seeking to share it with others or to worry about things. I AM one with God, and that is always enough.

5

PRAY, THEN, LIKE THIS

Pray then like this:
Our Father who art in heaven,
Hallowed be thy name.
Thy kingdom come.
Thy will be done,
 On earth as it is in heaven.
Give us this day our daily bread;
And forgive us our debts,
 As we also have forgiven our debtors;
And lead us not into temptation,
 But deliver us from evil.
For thine is the kingdom, and the power, and the glory, forever, Amen!

For if you forgive men their trespasses, your heavenly Father also will forgive you; but if you do not forgive men their trespasses, neither will your Father forgive your trespasses."

"Our Father . . ."

Having instructed us in how to pray, Jesus now offers a model prayer for us to use. The Lord's Prayer has become by far the best-known, most often used prayer in the world.

Many prayers are human-centered; that is, they beseech God to intervene in human life to provide something—health, success, happiness—which appears to be lacking.

The Lord's Prayer, however, is different. It is completely God-centered. It begins and ends with a consciousness that God does not *have* what we want, God *is* what we want.

Jesus here, as he so often does, refers to God with the Aramaic term "Abba." It is a child's word; it means not Father but Papa. It bespeaks an attitude that is intimate, loving, and trusting. It suggests a radically new relationship between God and humankind (not just Jesus, of course; after all, he's telling others to pray this way). This new relationship is different from the standard Judaism practiced by Jesus' first listeners and, indeed, different from that of normative Christianity in years to come; for many Christians later reverted to a more formal, distant, and fear-based sense of God.

MEDITATION

I am one with the Power of God that dwells within me. My Father, my true Source, is the indwelling Presence and Power of God. There is no distance, no separation, no "other" in my life. There is only God, expressing as me, in this day.

"Who art in heaven . . ."

And where is heaven? Jesus is quite clear: "The kingdom of heaven is within." Abba, then, this intimate Lord of our Being, is present within us, and heaven exists within us as a potential that once expressed will transform the world.

The idea that we are meant to prayerfully accept lives of limitation and pain in hopes of achieving "heaven" in a realm beyond death is not consistent with the teachings of Jesus, here or in any part of his ministry. The kingdom of heaven is not beyond death, or in the clouds, or around the next bend in the road. It is "at hand," Jesus said; it is "within." We have to know that it is within us and release its "imprisoned splendor" (to quote Robert Browning) with every choice we make. Then, and only then, will the kingdom of heaven come to pass. God the Source has placed its power and potential eternally within us. Jesus Christ has tried to help us remember its Presence within us through his teachings and demonstrations. The next step is ours to take.

MEDITATION

I dedicate this day to creating the kingdom in every area of my life. Every choice I make today will reflect the Presence of God within me. Thank You, God, for the energy of love and the gentle reminders that will help this day move me toward the kingdom!

"Hallowed be thy name . . ."

Throughout the scriptures of all great religions, the name of God is of supreme importance because in the sounds of the name can be found the power that God is. When Moses encountered God in a burning bush and asked His name, he was told, "I AM that I AM."

And so we are called to begin to pray by appreciating the loving presence of God within us as a power that releases and expresses when we speak forth the Word, the hallowed name, I AM.

MEDITATION

Today I will honor the Power of God's Presence within me, and I will choose carefully how I use the hallowed name. I do not choose to connect the "I AM" that represents God in me with any ideas of lack, limitation, weakness, or negative energy. Any statement that I begin with "I AM" I will complete with words of love, gratitude, and empowerment. Thank You, God!

"Thy kingdom come . . ."

This line is a perfect example of affirmative prayer. It does not beg or beseech, hoping that something might be true. It rather recognizes that God is constant, eternal, unchangeable. There is no need to ask for God's good; it is only important that we know and affirm that it is already with us.

The kingdom of God is at hand. It exists in potential within each one of us, as the Christ of our Being. "Thy kingdom come" affirms our willingness to allow this potential kingdom to manifest through our own creative cooperation.

God is eternally doing that which God does—creating the ideal of the kingdom and placing it within us. We hereby agree to do our part to bring forth the kingdom.

MEDITATION

Because I remember the truth of my oneness with God, the kingdom of heaven lives in my consciousness today. I give thanks in advance for every opportunity the day will bring to demonstrate my awareness of God within me and to bring the kingdom into expression around me. Thank You, God!

"Thy will be done, on earth as it is in heaven."

How, then, are we to bring about the kingdom? By expressing the order, guidance, goodness, and love of God in all of life.

All these aspects of the Presence and Power of God are already fully present in the kingdom of heaven, which, Jesus tells us, is within us. It is the Will of God that we be eternally supplied with all that God is; this indwelling Presence is what we call the Christ.

The process of expressing on earth this same divine perfection that exists within us, in potential form, is our creative work to do. We must first remember our oneness with God, rediscovering what the Apostle Paul called "the mystery hidden for ages and generations . . . Christ in you, the hope of glory (Col. 1:26-27)." We then begin to bring the kingdom of heaven to earth by bringing it first into our own being, so that each cell, each organ, each thought held in mind becomes an expression of God.

As we become one with the Christ within, so does the kingdom of God become one with the manifest world in which we live. Day by day, choice by choice, we are given abundant opportunities to create the kingdom by releasing the divine energy of God that lives within us. And this completion of the creative process is the very epitome of the Will of God. God's highest purpose is not to act upon us but to work through us.

MEDITATION

Today, through all the challenges, lessons, and opportunities of the day, I will remember always to affirm, "Thy will be done." I will express the Spirit of God within me in each choice, each challenge that the day may bring. This is my agreement with the Power of God to bring the perfection of heaven into my earthly life. Thank You, God, for each opportunity to express Your will on earth!

"Give us this day our daily bread."

The entire first half of the Lord's Prayer, then, is not about ourselves or our needs. It is simply a focus on the nature and power of God. We affirm God's Presence within us and our willingness to surrender to that Presence. It is from this elevated spiritual perspective, then, that we turn to our own life experience as the prayer continues.

The nourishment we receive from Spirit is often equated with the food necessary to sustain life. These words would have reminded Jesus' original listeners of the manna that appeared each day for the Israelites wandering in the wilderness; they might also have thought of the ways in which Elijah was nourished in the course of his prophetic work. Later in the gospels we will find these words echoed in Jesus' own feeding of 5,000 and in his frequent assurances that the loving energy of God will joyfully supply all our needs if we are willing to allow that to happen.

Give us this day our daily bread. And our daily bread does not signify a diet of scant sufficiency. "It is the Father's good pleasure to give you the kingdom," Jesus said. It is our job to accept that kingdom, accept the daily bread of abundance, love, guidance, and perfect health that is our gift from God. It is *our* daily bread by virtue of our oneness with God. We claim our inheritance and the spiritual nourishment, the power it represents.

MEDITATION

Today I will be alert and grateful as I recognize the many ways in which I am fed by Spirit. I am, now and always, nourished by the indwelling Presence of God, and I welcome each opportunity this day will bring to feed and nourish others through words of love, respect, and appreciation. Thank You, God!

"Forgive us our debts, as we also have forgiven our debtors."

Jesus spoke in Aramaic, and so presumably the entire Sermon on the Mount was originally phrased in that subtle, poetic language with its roots in both Arabic and Hebrew. English translations have largely been based on the Greek Septuagint or Latin Vulgate versions, which were themselves translated from the Aramaic original. Through such multiple translations, many fine points and important nuances can be obscured through error and misunderstanding.

This has been particularly true in the case of this line from the Lord's Prayer. Most accurately translated, it reads as above: Forgive us our debts as we also have forgiven our debtors.

To convey the true sense of the original, we need to think of debts not as the accounts payable of Western understanding, but in an Eastern sense of karma. Karmic debts are the residue left from negative choices we have made in the past, in this life or another. Science tells us that for every action there is an equal and opposite reaction. Any action based on fear, lack, or limitation produces a karmic debt to ourselves or to another.

The verb tense is important here. "We also have forgiven our debtors." It suggests that we must have already released any sense of debt owed to us before we can begin to ask God to forgive our own sense of debt.

Spiritually speaking, a consciousness of debt is a consciousness of resentment and victimization. I resent others for perceived offenses, and I feel myself victimized by the actions and attitudes of others in my life experience. I feel paralyzed by this sense of debt; I can be of no assistance in the work of creating the kingdom as long as I feel personally powerless, waiting for others to pay their perceived debts.

And what does it mean to forgive a debt? Certainly it suggests more than simply wiping a slate clean. It requires us to recognize that no indebtedness could ever truly happen in a world that is an expression of the love and abundance of God. If we maintain that awareness in our interactions with others, we can be sure that the Presence and Power of God will respond with a constant flow of forgiving love through us. We will always be forgiven our debts as long as we keep our own channels of forgiveness open and clear.

MEDITATION

Today I affirm that mine is a life of perfect abundance, because the Presence of God flows through me. I erase every sense of lack from my life, and I dissolve every resentment against others whom I wrongly perceived to be blocking my good. As I forgive myself and others, I feel God's love filling my being and overflowing into all my life. Thank You, God!

"And lead us not into temptation, but deliver us from evil."

Even as a young altar boy, I never understood the idea that God might lead us into temptation. Unity co-founder Charles Fillmore, seeking a more accurate sense of the Aramaic, renders it as *"Leave* us not *in* temptation," and this makes more sense to me. It suggests that, while we may have wandered into temptation on our own, we can and do evoke the Presence of God within us to guide us safely back to our true spiritual home.

Ramakrishna, the great nineteenth-century Indian mystic, compared God as Divine Mother to a mortal mother who gives her child toys with which to amuse himself or herself while the mother goes about her work. We, too, Ramakrishna said, "have been distracted by toys, the bright baubles that represent the things of the world. Only when we are able and willing to relinquish our toys for a time can we focus instead on the work of Divine Mother, a work that is ours to share and inherit."

Evil is simply another name for ignorance of God's Law, ignorance of our own spiritual identity, ignorance of the creative process that is the essence of our relationship with God and the dynamic behind our role in transforming human life into the kingdom of heaven. We are delivered from evil when we awaken to the truth: we are not powerless victims, but empowered creators, one with God and with each other, joined in the great spiritual work of bringing the kingdom of heaven into expression on earth.

MEDITATION

Today I feel the Power of God within me, lovingly leading me away from all temptation. I am delivered from all thoughts and impulses based on ignorance of my spiritual purpose and power. I am one with God, an instrument for love and forgiveness in every situation. My life is whole and perfect, and the kingdom of heaven is expressing through me now. Thank You, God!

"For thine is the kingdom, and the power, and the glory, forever, Amen!"

Apparently added as an afterthought by a spiritually moved scribe who was copying the gospels in the early years of the Christian Era, this doxology that often ends the Lord's Prayer is nonetheless an effective closing, since it returns our focus from self to God and opens new doors of possibility in our lives.

To recognize the Presence and Power of God as the truth of our being is empowering and exciting; but it must always be kept in divine perspective. It is true and important to realize that we are one with all that God is; but that does not mean that we are God.

I could easily go to the coast with an empty glass and fill it with water from the ocean. It would be accurate and important to recognize that the water in the glass is one with the ocean, in that it contains all the necessary elements. But to say that the glass of water is the Pacific Ocean is to ignore the vast and powerful totality of the larger entity. This is not a perfect analogy, since nothing has ever separated us from the Allness of God the way the glass separates the waters. Our relationship to God is more like that of a fish to the ocean in which it lives: God is the energy of everything that is.

And so, while we spend much of the Lord's Prayer affirming and accepting our own creative role in bringing the kingdom of heaven onto earth, it is fitting and important that we close by recognizing that while we are a part of all that is, we are not the Source of all that is. There is a dimension to God that transcends and, indeed, creates our own spiritual energy. In wonder and gratitude, we conclude this empowering prayer by dissolving our own spiritual energy into the All.

MEDITATION

I spend this day appreciating God as the energy of all life, expressing everywhere. The abundance in my life is God's kingdom in expression. The love and creativity in my life are God's power in expression. The beauty and joy in my life are God's glory in expression. I am one with all that God is, and I am grateful! Thank You, God!

"For if you forgive men their trespasses, your heavenly Father also will forgive you. But if you do not forgive men their trespasses, neither will your Father forgive your trespasses."

Again and again, not just in the Sermon on the Mount but in all his teachings, Jesus emphasizes the importance of forgiveness. Again and again He emphasizes that we cannot receive from the Christ of our Being anything we are not willing to share freely with all others, even, or especially, our apparent enemies.

"Love your enemies," Jesus advises. "Do good to those who persecute you." This is often interpreted as moralistic advice, but in fact it is extremely practical. Forgiveness is not just a good thing; it is the key of access to the divine laws, according to which the Presence and Power of God express in our lives and in our world. To fully feel God's love in our lives, we must extend God's love to all others. Conversely, every instance of resentment or unforgiveness toward others causes us to feel more alone, separate from others and from the Presence of God.

We can see the same law at work in every area of life. In prosperity, for example, we learn that it is by allowing abundance to express through us to others that we can most fully experience our own indwelling prosperity. Here what we forgive is every sense of lack or limitation.

In all of our lives, the extent to which we believe that any individual deserves less than God's perfect expression of Good is the extent to which we deprive ourselves of that same Good. And the extent to which we heal our vision and see others as love expressing is the extent to which we experience the Presence of God in our own lives.

MEDITATION

Today I recognize that the only obstacles blocking the perfect expression of God in my life are of my own making. To every challenge that appears on my path today, I ask only: What have I not forgiven? As old resentments and negative judgments, of myself and others, come to mind, I gently dissolve them in my newfound awareness of God's love within me. As I forgive, I am forgiven, and my life is blessed. Thank You, God!

6

LIVING A LIFE

And when you fast, do not look dismal, like the hypocrites, for they disfigure their faces that their fasting may be seen by men. Truly, I say to you, they have received their reward. But when you fast, anoint your head and wash your face, that your fasting may not be seen by men but by your Father who is in secret; and your Father who sees in secret will reward you.

"Do not lay up for yourselves treasures on earth, where moth and rust consume and where thieves break in and steal, but lay up for yourselves treasures in heaven, whether neither moth nor rust consumes, and where thieves do not break in and steal. For where your treasure is, there will your heart be also.

"The eye is the lamp of the body. So, if your eye is sound, your whole body will be full of light; but if your eye is not sound, your whole body will be full of darkness. If, then, the light in you is darkness, how great is the darkness!

"No one can serve two masters; for either he will hate the one and love the other, or he will be devoted to the one and despise the other. You cannot serve God and mammon.

"Therefore I tell you, do not be anxious about your life, what you shall eat or what you shall drink, nor about your body, what you shall put on. Is not life more than food, and the body more than clothing? Look at the birds of the air: they neither sow nor reap nor gather into barns, and yet your heavenly Father feeds them. Are you not of more value than they? And which of you, by being anxious, can add one cubit to his span of life? And why are you anxious about clothing? Consider the lilies of the field, how they grow; they neither toil nor spin; yet I tell you, even Solomon in all his glory was not arrayed like one of these. But if God so clothes the grass of the field, which today is alive and tomorrow is thrown into the oven, will he not much more clothe you, O men of little faith? Therefore do not be anxious, saying 'What shall we eat?' or 'What shall we drink?' or 'What shall we wear?' For the Gentiles seek all these things; and your heavenly Father knows that you need them all. But seek first His kingdom and His righteousness, and all these things shall be yours as well.

"Therefore do not be anxious about tomorrow, for tomorrow will be anxious for itself. Let the day's own troubles be sufficient for the day."

"And when you fast, do not look dismal like the hypocrites, for they disfigure their faces that their fasting may be seen by men. Truly, I say to you, they have received their reward. But when you fast, anoint your head and wash your face, that your fasting may not be seen by men but by your Father who is in secret. And your Father who sees in secret will reward you."

As we continue to move through the Sermon on the Mount, we find that Jesus emphasizes the importance of certain teachings by repeating them several times in different contexts.

He has already advised his followers that prayer should not be done publicly, to impress others, but secretly, to connect us with God. He now tells us that the same divine Law applies to other religious observances as well.

There are two important elements to this teaching. One we've discussed twice. It is that in prayer, in tithing, in fasting, in all activities that we choose to call good, our reward will be where we focus. If we do good simply to impress others, that will be our only reward. We may, indeed, impress others. But no spiritual benefit will accrue. If we do good quietly, privately, solely to know God, then that will be our reward. And having put God first, we can be sure that all other rewards will follow.

The second element in this teaching is equally important. It is simply that the spiritual path is not meant to be sorrowful, depressing, or sacrificial. Feeling God's Presence within us should be the greatest of joys. Those people who insist on acting as if God prefers poverty, sadness, and solemnity are, in Jesus' word, hypocrites. The word translated as "hypocrite" means "actor," and that's exactly what such people are. They are pretending to a level of spiritual depth that they cannot understand and have never truly experienced. They are missing the point, and they are not to be trusted as spiritual examples.

MEDITATION

Today I will let my face and manner express my spiritual joy. I will choose today, not to impress others, but to love them unconditionally, as the expression of God that I am. Thank You, God, for the private joy of your Presence and Power within me.

"Do not lay up for yourselves treasure on earth, where moth and rust consume and thieves break in and steal, but lay up for yourselves treasure in heaven, where neither moth nor rust consumes, and where thieves do not break in and steal. For where your treasure is, there will your heart be also."

In this beautiful and powerful passage, Jesus carefully and patiently explains everything we need to know about abundance, about the perils and possibilities of our co-creative role with the Presence and Power of God.

"Lay up for yourselves treasure in heaven." And the kingdom of heaven, Jesus told us, is within. The treasure itself is not so important. But what we choose to see as treasure, and where we see it, will determine where we focus our heart. And our heart energy represents the indwelling Presence of God, the Christ of our Being.

If we place our heart upon external treasure, we will certainly accumulate treasure. But it will not last. It will be damaged, destroyed, lost, or stolen by enemies and thieves in the external, physical realm.

But if it is an internal treasure of love, faith, peace, order, and wisdom that speaks to our heart, then those qualities and all other divine ideas will grow stronger and richer within us. And since they are all rooted in God, they cannot be lost or destroyed. They are ours forever.

MEDITATION

Today I will carefully choose my goals and values, placing the enormous power of my heart behind every inner treasure that is God within me, knowing that all treasure, and all good besides, is now mine forever. Thank You, God!

"The eye is the lamp of the body. So if your eye is sound, your whole body will be full of light. But if your eye is not sound, your whole body will be full of darkness. If, then, the light in you is darkness, how great is the darkness!"

Throughout this close appreciation of the Sermon on the Mount, we have been using the Revised Standard Version—the RSV translation of the New Testament. This is a rare instance where the renowned Authorized (King James) Version seems not only more powerful and beautiful (which is often the case) but also more expressive of Jesus' metaphysical meaning.

In the King James translation, what Jesus says is this: **"If therefore thine eye be single, thy whole body shall be filled with light."**

The eye—singular—is the lamp of the body. What Jesus calls the "eye" is the source of light, of energy. It is the power in which we place our faith.

When we rely on the evidence of our senses—our double eyes of mortal sight—we are drawing from an energy of duality. We are believing sensory evidence that insists we are separate from each other and from God. When our eye is single, we are relying on the unified light of the Christ Presence within us. We recognize One Presence, One Power. We see clearly, because we see only God in expression wherever we look.

MEDITATION

Today, I pray, "Let mine eye be single." Let me see only God, let the light within me flow from God's Presence and Power within me. Let me feel the light of God expressing in and through every cell of my body. It is my right and obligation to choose the lamp that will light my being. Today I choose the single light of God. Thank You, God!

"No one can serve two masters. For either he will hate the one and love the other, or he will be devoted to the one and despise the other. You cannot serve God and mammon."

Jesus' teaching in this passage from the Sermon on the Mount is simply a new perspective on the oldest of all the laws in the Hebrew Bible. "I AM the Lord, your God," Moses is given as the First Commandment. "You shall have no strange gods before me." No one can serve two masters—not because it's wrong, but because it can't be done. Since, according to spiritual law, we create according to where we place the perceiving power of our mind, to serve two masters would be to create a dualistic reality, which cannot have firm anchor in Truth.

It might be tempting to believe that this has no relevance to us today. We are not idol-worshippers; we do not serve other gods. But, of course, we do.

What is the second master we try to serve? What is our false god? It may be money, success, status. It may be a relationship. It may be pleasure, or a particular cause, or any of our possible addictions.

Whatever it is, this teaching of Jesus is essential to our own spiritual development. We are to put God first. We are to resist the temptation to balance our spiritual commitment with other, more materialistic concerns. If balance is needed, we can be sure that the Presence and Power of God will provide that balance. Our job is to choose one master to serve. Joshua recognized this truth early in the Hebrew Bible, in his final address to the Israelites he has just led into their Promised Land. "Choose this day who you will serve," he tells the assembled tribes. "But as for me and my family, we serve the Lord!"

MEDITATION

Today, I affirm that my eye is single and I serve but one master. That master is the Lord of my being, the Presence of God guiding and supporting me through this life experience. Thank You, God!

"Therefore I tell you, do not be anxious about your life, what you shall eat or what you shall drink, nor about your body, what you shall put on. Is not life more than food, and the body more than clothing?"

This begins perhaps the greatest and most exciting affirmation of Jesus' ministry, a passionate promise that there is nothing to fear. It's quoted often, but it has come to be regarded simply as a beautiful metaphor. For nearly 2,000 years people have studiously ignored the possibility that Jesus meant exactly what he said.

"Do not be anxious about your life." This would be a great assurance if it were intended for an individual who had lived an exemplary life, a life that the rest of us judged to be "good." For such a person, this is the kind of reward we would expect God to offer.

But Jesus is not speaking here to one perfect person. He is speaking to His disciples and through them to all mankind. He is stating unequivocally that there is no reason for any person to be anxious about life.

This is not a flowery figure of speech. It is a plain and simple directive that happens to go against the collective consciousness of the world, particularly today, when anxiety seems to be the very nature of life.

We will see as we continue through this section of the Sermon on the Mount that Jesus has much more to say in addressing this point. But it's important to see the clear statement with which He begins: "Do not be anxious about your life."

MEDITATION

Today I will gently resist every temptation to feel anxious about any issue, challenge, or relationship in my life. I rest in the certainty of my oneness with God, and I am at peace. Thank You, God!

"Look at the birds of the air: they neither sow nor reap nor gather into barns, and yet your heavenly Father feeds them. Are you not of more value than they?"

Humans are the only creatures on the planet who do not implicitly accept the benevolent energy of God. We pretty much invented the whole concept of stress, although we've managed to impose it on some of our closest fellow creatures along the way.

Jesus is not using the example of the birds as a general figure of speech. He means us to seriously consider what He's saying. "Look," He says, "at the birds of the air." Birds do not spend their lives worrying about how they will be fed. They do not feel that they are alone in a remorseless world, forced to fend for themselves. When they are hungry they seek food, and they find it. It never occurs to them that they won't.

The same is true of all creatures in the wild. Yes, life may be harsh; food may be scarce, or drought may dry up their source of water. But they accept their roles in the circle of life; they don't blame God or themselves. They do what they need to do in order to eat and feed their young; beyond that, they relax, accept, enjoy.

Our spiritual purpose, of course, is higher. In the rich and wonderful story told in chapters 2 and 3 of the Book of Genesis, it is humankind that undertakes the experience of Good and Evil symbolized by the apple. We are thus the only creatures to whom it occurs that God might be absent, that we might need to compete among ourselves for limited supplies.

Jesus is suggesting that logic alone should help us see the fallacy of this line of thinking. We are precious and important to the Power of God precisely because we agreed to enter into an experience of duality, in order to learn to make the choices that will transform it into the kingdom of heaven. Is it logical to believe that whereas lesser creatures are able to experience life in trust and appreciation, we are somehow an exception to God's love?

Too many people through the centuries have claimed in Jesus' name that we are "sinners in the hands of an angry God," that God indeed nourishes all of life but us, because we were disobedient. Nothing in the ministry of Jesus justifies that idea. Moving into this dualistic experience was not an act of spiritual disobedience but of spiritual courage and willingness. It did not cause the Power of God to reject us but to embrace us as its own creative expression.

It only stands to reason, therefore, that the Power of God at work in all creation will enfold and sustain us. We still have our work to do, just as the birds of the air have to search for their nourishment. But we, too, are part of the circle of life; we are always within God's loving care, and there is nothing to fear.

MEDITATION

I am, today and always, immersed in the nourishing love of God. I choose to see and appreciate the many ways in which my needs are met, my life made richer and more joyous, through the Power of God expressing everywhere. Thank You, God, for Your eternal love and support.

"And which of you by being anxious can add one cubit to his span of life? And why are you anxious about clothing? Consider the lilies of the field, how they grow; they neither toil nor spin; yet I tell you, even Solomon in all his glory was not arrayed like one of these. But if God so clothes the grass of the field, which today is alive and tomorrow is thrown into the oven, will He not much more clothe you, O men of little faith?"

Clearly it was extremely important to Jesus that His followers understand this central teaching about the omnipresent Power of God. It's easy to see why. If we don't understand that we need not focus all our energy and attention on questions of survival and comfort, we will never feel ourselves free to explore and express our greater spiritual purpose.

Anxiety serves no purpose. There may be no single teaching of Jesus more needed in today's world than this. If I am stuck in a traffic jam, I have two choices. I can be angry and anxious, fuming at the delay and worrying about its effect on my life. Or I can relax, meditate, listen to music, plan my day, and accept a situation that I have no power to control. The first choice will not get me on my way any faster, but it *will* damage my physical well-being, tie my emotions up in knots, and introduce the paralysis of stress into my mental abilities. What's the point?

Like the lilies of the field, we are perfect just as we are. We do not need to *become* anything more than we already are. In fact, we have never even remotely begun to appreciate our own indwelling beauty. We do not need to go anywhere or do anything to experience God's love and abundance in our lives. We must simply become men and women of great faith—faith in God and faith in ourselves.

MEDITATION

Today I choose to do what once would have seemed impossible: I will live this day without anxiety or stress. I will see every challenge as an opportunity to affirm that I am one with God. My happiness and prosperity are assured, and there is nothing to fear. Thank You, God!

"Therefore do not be anxious, saying, 'What shall we eat?' or 'What shall we drink?' or 'What shall we wear?' For the Gentiles seek all these things, and your heavenly Father knows that you need them all."

We would not use the term "Gentile" today with the same meaning that Jesus intended it to have, but the people he so describes are still with us. Indeed, we have all been "Gentiles" in Jesus' sense of the word. He is referring to those who do not believe, who are not aware of the spiritual dimension of life.

We cannot live spiritual lives if we continue to adopt without question the values and assumptions of our old, faithless existence. This is an important and subtle point. It is depicted in the life of Jesus in the stories of His time in the wilderness, beset by temptations to misuse the spiritual power He had come to teach and demonstrate. The "Satan" of fear-based thinking wants Him to use his powers to achieve abundance, fame, and power, to solve the very problems that have always consumed human energy and attention.

But Jesus knows then, and teaches now, that this will not work. We cannot simply use faith to solve the problems of fear; we must recognize that in our new spiritual awareness there is nothing to fear. We do not use spiritual awareness to solve our problems; we surrender to the awareness of God within us, and our problems dissolve like the illusions they have always been.

MEDITATION

Today I know and affirm that God does not have what I want. God ***is*** *what I want. I spend this day in constant awareness of God's eternal Presence within me, and I give thanks for the peace and abundance I feel.*

"But seek first His kingdom and His righteousness, and all these things shall be yours as well."

Here is the simple secret of a life well-lived, expressed as clearly and succinctly as it could ever be. If nothing survived of the teachings of Jesus but this one sentence, he would still stand as our greatest teacher.

Put God first, rigorously and without exception, and everything—everything!—we need in our lives will be given to us. Put God first. Make expressing the kingdom of God the first priority in every situation.

And if we do that with all our heart and mind, if we lovingly refuse to entertain any fearful thoughts of lack or insufficiency, if we overcome our human tendency to believe that we have to feed and clothe ourselves or we will starve and freeze and perish, then and only then will we begin to catch a glimmer of God's eager, joyful, and limitless love for us.

It is not a love that asks us to do without the pleasures of life. It is a love that asks us to keep our priorities clear and our focus always on the Presence of God within us. As we do that, we will receive more joy and abundance than we have ever imagined. But if we make the joy and abundance our focus and purpose, we will be back in a life experience of stress, fear, and poverty. Put God first.

MEDITATION

Today I joyfully put God first in every moment, every corner of my life. I want only to feel my oneness with God in every circumstance and situation. I put God first, and I give thanks for the heart-centered peace I feel as a result. Thank You, God!

"Therefore do not be anxious about tomorrow, for tomorrow will be anxious for itself. Let the day's own trouble be sufficient for the day."

Having encouraged his followers to seek first the kingdom, assured that all things on the material plane will be added as long as the kingdom, and the kingdom alone, is our primary purpose, Jesus next urges freedom from another great source of anxiety.

We are told in the spiritual study known as *A Course in Miracles* that "now" is the only moment of time that exists in eternity. We are also told that our ideas of "past" and "future" are the greatest barriers we have erected to a full appreciation of our true identity as eternal spiritual beings. Old tapes of guilt and resentment over the past and anxiety and stress about the future both pull us off center.

We're all familiar with Fleetwood Mac's popular advice that we "Don't stop thinking about tomorrow." It might be more appropriate to sing, "Don't *start* thinking about tomorrow." Each moment is a self-contained unit of spiritual possibility. Staying in the eternal Now keeps us centered in our hearts, free of stress about past or future.

MEDITATION

"Do not be anxious about tomorrow." Today, all day, I will remember to stay in today. Centered in my heart, I have in abundance all the energy I will need for the lessons of today. I release the past. I release the future. I live in today, and I am abundantly supplied. Thank You, God!

Live the life
you fear -

define your fears
before your goals

all that shapelessness
is dangerous.

7

THE HEART OF THE MATTER

Judge not, that you be not judged. For with the judgment you pronounce you will be judged, and the measure you give will be the measure you get. Why do you see the speck that is in your brother's eye, but do not notice the log that is in your own eye? Or how can you say to your brother, 'Let me take the speck out of your eye,' when there is the log in your own eye? You hypocrite, first take the log out of your own eye, and then you will see clearly to take the speck out of your brother's eye.

"Do not give dogs what is holy; and do not throw your pearls before swine, lest they trample them under foot and turn to attack you."

"Judge not, that you be not judged. For with the judgment you pronounce you will be judged, and the measure you give will be the measure you get."

Stress is our major planetary challenge today, whether on a personal, national, or global scale. And unnecessary judgment is the major cause of stress. All stress. We literally wear ourselves out with the energy we expend judging everything and everyone throughout every day. We look at people, things, events in the outer world and we decide to blame them for our perceived lacks—of abundance, or security, or love or health—in short, for all the challenges of our life experience. We forget or ignore the fact that those other people, things, events simply mirror our own consciousness. So, as Jesus points out in this important passage, we are always really judging ourselves. **"For with the judgment you pronounce you will be judged, and the measure you give will be the measure you get."**

The fruit of judgment is the trap of *victimization.* We are helpless victims—of others, of our own past, of our addictions to negative choice. We may even choose to see ourselves as victims of the very spiritual Law that Jesus is trying to help us understand. "It's how it is! It's how I am! It's how God is! Alas! Poor me!"

I think the entire Sermon on the Mount could be distilled down to these two sentences. If we truly stop judging ourselves and others, we will find our lives transformed. We will realize that through the whole process of judgment, we have done far more harm to ourselves than we could ever hope to do to those we've been negatively judging. We will discover a sense of freedom and an abundance of energy to devote to more joyful, spiritually empowering things. We will instinctively be more loving to others, and we will immediately find more love expressing in our lives as well, according to the simple, profound, and absolute promise that Jesus teaches.

MEDITATION

Today I resolve to recognize every temptation to judge, freezing the moment, taking it to my heart, and enfolding it in the energy of God I find there. I affirm that by extending that heart energy to others, I will experience it tenfold in my own life. Thank You, God!

"Why do you see the speck in your neighbor's eye, but do not notice the log in your own eye? Or how can you say to your neighbor, 'Let me take the speck out of your eye,' while the log is in your own eye? You hypocrite, first take the log out of your own eye, and then you will see clearly to take the speck out of your neighbor's eye."

We don't usually think of Jesus as a great stand-up comic, but it's clear, not just here but throughout the gospels, that he had a rich sense of humor—gentle, and always loving, but nonetheless reflecting the absurdity of our false beliefs and fear-based attitudes.

Jesus worked within an oral tradition, of course, and outrageous exaggeration is a time-honored way of helping listeners remember what they're being told. Certainly his followers would have laughed when they called to mind the image of a man with a log in his eye!

The comic image emphasizes and illustrates the directive against judgment in the preceding sentences. Clearly it was a point that Jesus wanted his listeners, and by extension us, to remember clearly.

Everything our senses report to us is warped by the distortions of our humanity. We can easily see those distortions in someone else's life. But it's important, and tricky, to remember that our own perceptions are equally warped. Our only spiritual purpose is to help others find and express their own indwelling Christ, their oneness with the Light and Love of God. It may seem like a mammoth task, but in fact it's like brushing away cobwebs or gently removing a speck from another's eye. The Allness of God is so great that the adjustment doesn't require a major transplant or a painful gouging. Just a loving flick will accomplish it.

But we must be able to see clearly through our own eyes before we can offer loving support to others. That "log" that Jesus so vividly describes in our own eye is sanctimoniousness and the distortion of judgment. It is the arrogance of presuming to point out the flaws of others before we have done anything about removing our own.

Jesus uses the word "hypocrite" frequently, especially in the Gospel according to Matthew. Because of its biblical connotations, it has taken on a deeply negative meaning through the years. In fact, though, it is from the Greek term for "actor." It simply suggests that we may find ourselves playing a pious role, going through the appropriate motions, rather than establishing a genuine connection with the Spirit of God within. Such play-acting cannot allow us to create the kingdom of heaven, and that, as Jesus repeatedly assures us, is our only purpose as spiritual beings sharing a human experience.

MEDITATION

My purpose today is to bring more of the kingdom of heaven into expression in my life. I begin by centering myself in the energy of God at the heart of my being, and brushing away any distortions in my consciousness caused by fear or old attitudes. I am then available to follow my inner guidance as I interact with others throughout the day, seeing and responding to only the Presence of God within each. Thank You, God!

"Do not give dogs what is holy, and do not throw your pearls before swine, lest they trample them underfoot and turn to attack you."

Jesus warns us frequently during His ministry that the path of spiritual awakening and spiritual transformation is often challenging. Nowhere is this more true than in our relationships with other people. To follow the example of Jesus may require that we leave behind father, mother, sister, brother—all those to whom we are tied in the old understanding.

It may seem a cruel paradox that this new path of love and healing may lead to painful separations, but it is simply the outpicturing of the Law. One person's spiritual journey, once begun, cannot be halted or delayed because someone else does not recognize its value. At least the journey cannot be halted without great pain and confusion.

The Power of God, the Christ, is present in every person. But not every person is able or willing to remember and recognize that Presence at any given moment. In this teaching from the Sermon on the Mount, Jesus is advising us not to waste energy and effort trying to share with the unawakened the joys of the spiritual path. This is not to say, of course, that we may not share with them on other levels, without trying to include them on a path that is not theirs.

In a later parable Jesus compares the kingdom of heaven to a pearl of great price. How foolish to find such a pearl and then throw it before swine, who will trample it underfoot and then attack you for not giving them something they could use, like food. It's important to note that the swine are not evil. They are perfectly expressing their nature. As with so many teachings, Jesus is talking not of morality but of efficiency.

MEDITATION

Today I am grateful for the clear, efficient path to the kingdom of heaven expressing from within me—and for the joyful company and community of other awakened spiritual beings. Thank You, God!

8

THE GREAT PROMISE

Ask, and it will be given you; seek, and you will find; knock, and it will be opened to you. For everyone who asks receives, and he who seeks finds, and to him who knocks it will be opened. Or what man of you, if his son asks him for bread, will give him a stone? Or if he asks for a fish, will give him a serpent? If you then, who are evil, know how to give good gifts to your children, how much more will your Father who is in heaven give good things to those who ask him! So whatever you wish that men would do to you, do so to them; for this is the law and the prophets.

"Enter by the narrow gate; for the gate is wide and the way is easy that leads to destruction, and those who enter by it are many. For the gate is narrow and the way is hard that leads to life, and those who find it are few."

"Ask and it will be given you; seek and you will find; knock and it will be opened to you. For everyone who asks receives; and he who seeks finds; and to him who knocks it will be opened."

Our overview of the Sermon on the Mount brings us now to one of the greatest promises in all of scripture—great because it does not speak of a heavenly "someday" that may seem impossible to achieve. Rather, it speaks directly to the challenges and possibilities of our life experience today. It is an unconditional promise of God's good, and it has been ignored for far too long.

We often speak today of a need for commitment. We may even end a relationship because of a perceived lack of commitment on our part or on the part of another.

How much greater a commitment could there ever be than that contained in these ringing words of Jesus? Here is not a God of judgment, giving or withholding favors according to some unknowable whim. This God is consistent, clear, knowable. **"Ask and it will be given you. Seek and you will find. Knock and it will be opened to you."**

The variable in this straightforward explanation of the creative process is not God; it is us. Are we willing to ask, seek, knock in full faith that the Presence and Power of God cannot help but respond? Do we claim the good available to us as fully empowered expressions of God?

If so, then we will receive that for which we ask, seek, knock. It's the Law. However, if we doubt that the Law will work for us, then whatever we do or don't create will express the frustrating imperfection of our doubts.

MEDITATION

Today I choose to ask, seek, and knock at each challenge, each opportunity. And I accept the good that results in my life as a joyous expression of the Power and Love of God. Thank You, God.

"Or what man of you, if his son asks him for bread, will give him a stone? Or if he asks for a fish, will give him a serpent? If you, then, who are evil, know how to give good gifts to your children, how much more will your Father who is in heaven give good things to those who ask Him!"

The image of God as Father has become commonplace; it is one of the first religious images most of us learned. It was not nearly as common in the time when Jesus taught; and His particular understanding about what the relationship implied was very uncommon indeed.

The more usual image of God and man in Hebrew scripture was of God as king and the nation of Israel as unruly subjects. Similarly, when the image was shifted to God as Father, it was seen as an angry and authoritarian Father faced with ungrateful and disobedient children. The emphasis was not on love but on obedience—strict obedience to the Father's firm and specific rules.

Jesus teaches differently, and it must have astounded His first listeners. "Everyone who asks receives," He has just said. This was definitely not the spiritual understanding of the time. In order to receive anything from God, it was commonly believed, you had to *deserve* God's favor by scrupulously obeying every law. God was seen as more interested in punishing than in appreciating, and even though it was presented as for our own good, it didn't create a warm relationship.

Now comes Jesus, and He has a very different perspective. Even from our limited and faltering level of spiritual awareness, we are capable of great love for our children. We love to give them what they ask for. God is the very essence of unconditional love—love that is truly beyond our ability to comprehend. How can we think that God would stand in judgment or withhold our good? We are invited to understand God as a very personal, loving Father, eager to respond when we ask, seek, and knock.

MEDITATION

Today I will know that I am the beloved child of an infinitely loving God. In every circumstance of the day, I will know that God is acting for my greatest good, guiding me gently to my greatest happiness. Nothing can diminish God's love, and my heart is open to receive it fully. Thank You, God!

"So whatever you wish that men would do to you, do so to them; for this is the Law and the prophets."

Here Jesus sums up thousands of years of spiritual growth and awareness in one perfect directive. "The Law and the prophets" refers to the books of the Hebrew Bible, and Jesus is offering the ultimate condensed version of its hundreds of pages of struggles and advances.

This is, of course, the Golden Rule, more familiarly stated as "Do unto others as you would have others do unto you." Every spiritual belief system on the planet includes a variation on this teaching; it has become a bromide.

And yet, what would actually happen if the world began to live according to this simple guideline? We would achieve the kingdom of heaven in record time! We would be creating good for others, knowing that they were creating good for us in return. We would not be judging or resenting, because we would not want to be judged or resented. There would be nothing to forgive, for everything would be an expression of love.

One of my favorite affirmations from *A Course in Miracles* is also one of the simplest: I want the peace of God. Everyone wants the peace of God. And everyone will experience that peace, when they are ready to embrace this simple suggestion.

MEDITATION

I choose to consciously live this day according to the Golden Rule. With everyone I encounter today, I will ask myself what I would want to receive from me if I were the other person. And I will choose, speak, and respond, according to that awareness. Thank You, God, for the simple power of the Golden Rule.

"Enter by the narrow gate; for the gate is wide and the way is easy that leads to destruction, and those who enter by it are many. For the gate is narrow and the way is hard that leads to life, and those who find it are few."

A wide, open gate teeming with traffic may seem like an ideal entrance, or exit, on our spiritual journey. Certainly it is the way of choice for our sensory self, using pleasure, power, and the demands of our human appetites as guideposts along a wide and popular highway.

Sometimes, however, even in the midst of the bustle and excitement of the wide path, we sense that we may be missing something important, that there may be a more beautiful, meaningful, private, and personal path. "I, I chose the road less traveled," Robert Frost wrote, "and that has made all the difference."

There is a private path for each of us, as Jesus here assures us. It is not always easy to find and, once found, it is not for the faint-hearted. It is narrow and precipitous. In the Hindu scripture known as the *Katha Upanishad* we read, "Like the sharp edge of a razor, the sages say, is the path. Narrow it is and difficult to tread."

I think it's important to note where it's going, this narrow road that appeals to so few. It leads, Jesus says, to life. To life. It is a path that does not, as we might expect, lead us away from our human experience, but deeper into it—deeper into life, but life experienced from the fresh, loving, and unique perspective of Spirit.

MEDITATION

Today I will turn from the temptation to settle for the easy, popular path. I will choose instead the scenic route—narrow and bumpy sometimes, but rich in surprises and unexpected rewards. Thank You, God, for guiding me to the narrow path of spiritual possibility.

9

LAST WORDS AND WARNINGS

Beware of false prophets, who come to you in sheep's clothing but inwardly are ravenous wolves. You will know them by their fruits. Are grapes gathered from thorns, or figs from thistles? So, every sound tree bears good fruit, but the bad tree bears evil fruit. A sound tree cannot bear evil fruit, nor can a bad tree bear good fruit. Every tree that does not bear good fruit is cut down and thrown into the fire. Thus you will know them by their fruits.

"Not everyone who says to me, 'Lord, Lord,' shall enter the kingdom of heaven, but he who does the will of my Father who is in heaven. On that day many will say to me, 'Lord, Lord, did we not prophesy in your name, and cast out demons in your name, and do many works in your name?' And then will I declare to them, 'I never knew you; depart from me, you evildoers.'

"Everyone then who hears these words of mine and does them will be like a wise man who builds his house upon the rock; and the rain fell, and the floods came, and the winds blew and beat upon that house, but it did not fall, because it had been founded on the rock. And everyone who hears these words of mine and does not do them will be like a foolish man who built his house upon the sand; and the rain fell, and the floods came, and the winds blew and beat against that house, and it fell; and great was the fall of it."

"And when Jesus finished these sayings, the crowds were astonished at his teaching, for he taught them as one who had authority and not as their scribes."

"Beware of false prophets, who come to you in sheep's clothing but inwardly are ravenous wolves. You will know them by their fruits. Are grapes gathered from thorns, or figs from thistles? So every sound tree bears good fruit, but the bad tree bears evil fruit. A sound tree cannot bear evil fruit, nor can a bad tree bear good fruit. Every tree that does not bear good fruit is cut down and thrown into the fire. Thus you will know them by their fruits."

In the Sermon on the Mount, Jesus is calling us to a new level of spiritual commitment, a commitment based not on laws carved in stone or written on scrolls, but on our intimate awareness of the Presence of God within us.

Like anything new, such as driving a new car or learning a new skill, our new spiritual commitment may seem confusing at first. We may not always be sure we're getting it right; we may not know whether the guidance we're hearing is from God or from our own fearful, limited ego self.

At such times of confusion, many "prophets" may want to guide us, to tell us what God wants us to know. It can be tempting to let such outside authorities—individuals, groups, belief systems, even particular books—make choices on our behalf. But there is an inherent danger in choosing to allow someone else to make spiritual choices for us. We may be trusting a wolf in sheep's clothing; the damage done by misplaced trust may be infinitely greater than the difficulty of choosing for ourselves.

Not to worry, Jesus assures us. We can easily distinguish the true prophets from the false by the results of their teachings in our lives. True prophets will never claim for themselves aspects of God that truly reside within us all; they will always strive, as Jesus always did, to help us recognize the Presence of God within ourselves. If we feel empowered as a result of their teaching, left with a clearer understanding of our own intimate relationship to God, then the prophet is true and can be trusted. If the "fruit" of the teaching is to create a sense of dependence on the teacher, then the prophet is false, and caution is advised.

Of course, the fruit does not appear on the tree at once, but in its proper season. Jesus is encouraging us in this analogy to relax, reduce our level of stress, suspend judgment, and watch. We must not only choose, but be sensitive and alert to the results of our choices. If the fruits of our choices are uncomfortable, we can simply dissolve those choices and their results in the great energy of the universe that is God, and create a new reality, a new fruit tree, based on the Presence and Guidance of God within us.

MEDITATION

Today I release any anxiety about the choices I've made and the results, the fruit of those choices, now blossoming in my life. I know that I am never less than the beloved child of God, eternally free to choose again. Thank You, God.

"Not everyone who says to me 'Lord, Lord' shall enter the kingdom of heaven, but he who does the will of my Father who is in heaven. On that day many will say to me 'Lord, did we not prophesy in your name and cast out demons in your name and do many mighty works in your name?' And then will I declare to them 'I never knew you. Depart from me, you evildoers."

As Jesus draws near the end of his great discourse called The Sermon on the Mount, we realize he has offered a wide-ranging description of the process by which we work with the Power of God within us to create the kingdom of heaven. By recognizing the indwelling Presence and drawing upon it for every choice we make, we send the Power of God forward into expression as the kingdom. It's a rich, simple, and infinitely empowering process that requires only our awareness and conscious cooperation.

There are a few loose ends to be tied up, and one of them is the important paradox that it is possible to do all the apparently right things and still fall far short of the kingdom—hence these harsh words and a deliberately alarming scenario.

We may have a great intellectual understanding of the working of Spirit and even be able to effect some impressive demonstrations. But if we lose sight of the fact that it is not us but "the Father within that does the work," our understanding and work are in vain. We are evildoers, misleading others about the ways in which God expresses on earth. Again Jesus is reminding us that there is no room in the kingdom for hypocrisy—for acting as if we are spiritually centered while in fact our lives are still founded on fear.

We must simply make those choices that express our oneness with God and with each other. The Hindu teacher Swami Vivekananda wrote, "Do not stand on a high pedestal and take five cents in your hand and say 'Here, you poor man.' But be grateful that the poor man is there, so that by making a gift to him you are able to help yourself. It is not the receiver who is blest, but it is the giver."

MEDITATION

Today, I follow my inner spiritual guidance simply for the joy it brings. I appreciate each opportunity to experience God's love moving through me to others. Thank You, God!

"Everyone then who hears these words of mine and does them will be like a wise man who built his house upon the rock. And the rain fell, and the floods came, and the winds blew and beat upon that house. But it did not fall, because it had been built upon the rock. And everyone who hears these words of mine and does not do them will be like a foolish man who built his house upon the sand. And the rain fell, and the floods came, and the winds blew and beat upon that house, and it fell. And great was the fall of it."

In this final teaching from the Sermon on the Mount, Jesus creates another great image to emphasize the importance of action as a central element in any spiritual commitment.

Just as He said earlier that it was not enough to say "Lord, Lord," so is He here advising those who would follow Him that simply hearing the message without action is a shaky foundation for spiritual possibility. The storms and challenges of life will continue to rage, and a spiritual center based on words alone—on intellectual understanding—will not hold firm.

Action is required for a firm spiritual foundation. Allowing our new understanding to express in our lives deepens and stabilizes our commitment. The result is a firm spiritual foundation that can easily withstand the challenges of life.

MEDITATION

Today I affirm that I am open to every opportunity to put spiritual understanding into practice, to act on my newly perceived relationship to God. Through that willingness I claim and express the power and love necessary to transform each challenge into a holy experience. Thank You, God!

"And when Jesus finished these sayings, the crowds were astonished at His teaching, for He taught them as one who had authority, and not as one of their scribes."

Imagine what you might have felt to be in the crowd around Jesus, to hear these powerful words in the immediacy of His Presence. Who could fail to be transformed by such an experience?

Well, in fact, many of the people who were able to personally experience the ministry of Jesus *did* fail to be transformed. Many shrugged and went on with their lives, unaffected by the message. Others were perhaps disappointed at the lack of an overt political call to action. Still others might have nodded in agreement but lacked the energy to claim the Truth for themselves. Others who *did* recognize the radical implications of Jesus' words may have felt extremely threatened, setting in motion the energy of resistance to His message that eventually led to the death of the messenger.

The Power of God is all around us today, no matter where we are or what we're doing. The Presence of God is reflected in everything and everyone we see. But if we are not open, receptive, and willing, we will not see, we will not hear, we will not recognize, and it wouldn't matter if Jesus Himself returned to repeat his message in person. If we are not willing to surrender our fears, we will not be receptive to God's love.

The authority of Jesus is the authority of God; and it lives not just in Him, but in each of us as well. The crowds will always be astonished, but the message of truth will echo in each heart that opens to receive it.

MEDITATION

Today, I affirm that my heart is open and receptive. I see God wherever I look—especially within myself. I experience today as God, enjoying the day as me. Thank You, God!

EPILOGUE

We now have completed our journey through one of the most powerful spiritual teachings ever expressed. We've moved beyond the deceptively familiar words to discover that the Sermon on the Mount contains a power that can transform lives.

From Jesus Christ, through the Gospel of Matthew, we have received the essence of all spiritual understanding. Each of us is, by our very nature, a spiritual being. At that level of spirit we are one with each other and one with the Presence and Power of God.

As spiritual beings we are engaged in the experience of human life—an experience so intense and confusing that it often blocks our spiritual energy with fearful illusions of lack, limitation, and weakness. These negative images arise from the false belief that we are distant from God; the truth is that we are one with God through the Christ, the expression of all God is, that lives within us.

Our path out of fear and limitation is clear. We must first remember and embrace our true spiritual identity. Next we must lovingly dissolve all ideas, beliefs, and behavior patterns that are based on our former, fear-based consciousness. We can effectively accomplish this only through our relationships with others. By forgiving false beliefs in others, we dissolve them in ourselves as well.

The goal of this spiritual unfolding, Jesus teaches, is clear. It is to create the kingdom of heaven. As perfect expressions of the Power of God, we are creators, just as God is the Supreme Creator of all that is. When we fuel our creative energy from the Christ within us, making choices that flow from our unity with God, what we create in the manifest world is an expression of God. One choice at a time, we are creating the kingdom of heaven. The kingdom already exists in potential within us; our creative cooperation with the Power of God brings it into manifestation.

Through the power of prayerful focus, our daily meditations have helped us to move further along the path of spiritual awareness than we have ever been before. It's important to note, however, that the text we've been studying is from the very earliest days of Jesus' public ministry.

Our Master Teacher spent three more years living and demonstrating this spiritual truth. Understanding and believing are important, but more is required. We must now put our knowing faith to work. We must recognize each event, each relationship, each challenge in our lives as an opportunity to strengthen our spiritual commitment. We must set aside every temptation to judge others and to judge ourselves, simply centering ourselves each day in the unconditional love that links us to God.

There will be other teachers and other texts. They will speak to us powerfully at certain times and about specific issues. If they are true guides, they will always support the energy of the Sermon on the Mount, which means they will always support and advance our own personal connection to the Presence and Power of God.

And if we ever feel stuck, or lost, or confused, the Sermon on the Mount is always available to us, as a great beacon lighting our lives and guiding our progress. We will always be welcome on this special mountain, to rest and meditate, and to hear again and again the loving, challenging message of our greatest Teacher.

AUTHOR'S BIO

Ed Townley is a minister, ordained in 1991 by Unity School of Christianity. He has served congregations in Beaverton, Oregon, and Chicago, Illinois, and is currently an Associate Minister with Unity Church of Dallas, Texas. Widely recognized for his unique and powerful approach to the Bible and his emphasis on appreciating life as a challenging and rewarding journey of transformation and discovery, Rev. Ed is a popular speaker and teacher in churches, spiritual centers, and other venues throughout the world. His Sunday talks can be heard at www.unitydallas.org; and further information is available at www.edtownley.com.